The Catholic Handbook for
Visiting the Sick and Homebound

2007
Year C

LITURGY
TRAINING
PUBLICATIONS

This book is for Extraordinary Ministers of Holy Communion who visit the sick and homebound. We recognize that in some situations the person(s) they visit may not be able to receive Holy Communion. In such cases, please refer to the *Pastoral Care of the Sick: Visits to the Sick and Visits to a Sick Child* or the *Book of Blessings: Orders for the Blessing of the Sick*.

Nihil Obstat
Reverend Brian J. Fischer, STL
Censor Deputatus
March 28, 2006

Imprimatur
Reverend John F. Canary, DMIN
Vicar General
Archdiocese of Chicago
March 29, 2006

The *Nihil Obstat* and *Imprimatur* are official declarations that a book is free of doctrinal and moral error. No implication is contained therein that those who have granted the *Nihil Obstat* and *Imprimatur* agree with the content, opinions, or statements expressed. Nor do they assume any legal responsibility associated with publication.

Published with the approval of the Committee on the Liturgy, United States Conference of Catholic Bishops.

Inside art by Sister Mary Grace Thul, OP

LTP appreciates your comments and suggestions. E-mail us at CHVS@ltp.org.

THE CATHOLIC HANDBOOK FOR VISITING THE SICK AND HOMEBOUND © 2006 Archdiocese of Chicago: Liturgy Training Publications, 1800 North Hermitage Avenue, Chicago IL 60622; 1-800-933-1800, fax 1-800-933-7094, e-mail orders@ltp.org. All rights reserved. See our website at www.LTP.org.

Printed in the United States of America.

ISBN-10: 1-56854-504-5
ISBN-13: 978-1-56854-504-2
CHVS7

TABLE OF CONTENTS

Lent

Easter

Ordinary Time

Psalm 23

The Good Shepherd

The Lamb himself will be their shepherd and will lead them to the springs of living waters (Revelation 7:17)

The Lord is my shepherd;
there is nothing I shall want.
Fresh and green are the pastures
where he gives me repose.
Near restful waters he leads me,
to revive my drooping spirit.

He guides me along the right path;
he is true to his name.
If I should walk in the valley of darkness
no evil would I fear.
You are there with your crook and your staff;
with these you give me comfort.

You have prepared a banquet for me
in the sight of my foes.
My head you have anointed with oil;
my cup is overflowing.

Surely goodness and kindness shall follow me
all the days of my life.
In the Lord's own house shall I dwell
for ever and ever.

INTRODUCTION

Suffering wears a thousand faces, and every face is Christ's. When we suffer sickness or the harsher effects of aging, we cannot really understand the reasons, but we can choose the rock on which to stand. We are members of the Body of Christ. Christ our Head becomes present in our suffering; in our dying we share his death; his voyage through death to the glory of the Resurrection becomes our journey. In him, we are held securely in the face of the anxiety, fear, anger, guilt, and grief that sickness or aging can bring. In him, we can grow out of the small, even petty, focus on ourselves to which illness tempts us into the greatness of heart which is every Christian's destiny.

But we cannot do it alone. One of the deepest causes of suffering experienced by those whom sickness or aging confines to the narrow world of home, hospital, or geriatric facility is a sense of isolation. We may feel misunderstood, rejected, abandoned by the healthy world of which we were a part, even by those who love us, even by God. There is something "wrong" with us. We are no longer useful. We cause other people discomfort and inconvenience. We may know how we "ought" to pray in times of suffering, but we can't seem to do it. We can't even go to church.

Extraordinary Ministers of Holy Communion are sent to step across the moat that isolates the sufferers, bringing them the comfort of personal presence and prayer. The word *extraordinary* can be confusing. In this case, the Church uses it officially to distinguish between ordained bishops, priests, and deacons, who are the "ordinary" ministers of Communion, and specially commissioned laypeople who fill in the gaps, so to speak, when there are not enough ordinary ministers to give Communion to everyone at Mass or to take Communion to the homebound. The words *extraordinary* and *ordinary* as they are used here may strike us as odd because they recall a time when there were so many priests and deacons that there was no need for laypeople to take on this role. This handbook is specially designed for the use of Extraordinary Ministers of Communion (lay ministers), so it does not contain the rites for the sacraments of Penance or the Anointing of the Sick and the special blessings that can be administered only by the ordained priest.

You, as an Extraordinary Minister of Holy Communion to the sick and homebound, have been called to be a sign and a bridge. Sent by the parish, you are the living sign that the community of faith and worship has not forgotten its absent sick, its invisible elderly. Bearing Jesus Christ in the Blessed Sacrament, you are a sign that God is and wants to be with them. Praying with them as a representative of Christ living in the Church, you draw them back into conscious communion with the whole Body of Christ. They, and their caregivers, are not alone.

Yours is a great privilege and a great responsibility. Perhaps at times it will seem too great for you. But you also are not alone. Your call from God to serve as an Extraordinary Minister of Holy Communion has been recognized and confirmed by your local parish through the rite of commissioning in which your pastor has publicly named you a minister of the Church. The parish or diocese provides a program that prepares you to exercise your ministry faithfully and effectively. The Church has provided an official book containing a wealth of rites for those who visit, pray with, and bring Communion to the sick or aging, especially those cut off from participation in the Sunday Mass.

The book is called *Pastoral Care of the Sick;* however, what you have in your hand, *The Catholic Handbook for Visiting the*

Sick and Homebound 2007, is a booklet containing selections of the official rites approved for use by laypeople. You will be able to use this book when you are sent to take Communion to other parishioners who are confined to their homes, hospitals, or geriatric centers. The most important resource you have as a minister, though, is your personal relationship with Christ, our healer and Savior. You too are the face of Christ.

USING THIS BOOK

The Catholic Handbook for Visiting the Sick and Homebound will tell you what the Church asks of you as our spokesperson to say and do when you take Communion to the sick and aging who can't take part in Sunday Mass. You need not worry about "making up prayers"—here they are! In fact, you *should* use the prayers as they are written because they express the common faith of the Catholic Church to which we all committed ourselves in Baptism. We are called to help one another to grow into the full breadth and depth of that faith. When you pray in the name of the Church you represent, you are asking the sick and others who gather with them to say, "Amen"; that is, "Yes, I agree, I will abide by that, and I want God to do what you are asking in our name." By substituting other prayers, even if they are very deep and very beautiful, or even familiar Catholic prayers, you are silencing the words Christ has chosen to say through the Church at this particular time.

THE CONTENTS OF THE BOOK
THE RITES OF COMMUNION

This book provides two rites for lay ministers to give Communion to the sick. The first form, called Communion in Ordinary Circumstances, is especially useful if you are taking Communion to the sick or aging in their homes. It assumes two things: first, that you have enough time to lead the full rite of Holy Communion, including a short Liturgy of the Word; second, that those you visit are well enough to participate in a full service. The Church urges us always to consider the needs of the sick or aging. If they are very weak or tire quickly, it's better to shorten or omit elements like the explanation after the reading or the General Intercessions, or simply to use the shorter form called Communion in a Hospital or Institution even in a home setting.

This second form, Communion in a Hospital or Institution, provides a minimal format mainly intended for use when you are visiting many patients individually in an institutional setting. The Church expresses a strong preference for avoiding this abbreviated format even in an institution. Instead, it is suggested that if possible, you gather several residents together in one or more areas and celebrate the full rite of Communion in Ordinary Circumstances. If that is not possible, the Church recommends that you add elements from the fuller rite, such as the reading of the word, unless participants are too weak. On the other hand, in the case of extremely sick people, you may shorten even the rite for Communion in a Hospital or Institution by omitting as much of the rite as necessary. Try to include at least a greeting, the Lord's Prayer, the customary responses that precede Communion itself, and the closing prayer.

Both rites are simple to follow. Look them over before making your visits in order to familiarize yourself with the order of prayer. Directions are included and parts are clearly marked so that you can easily lead the communicants in prayer. Don't worry about differentiating between your role as a lay minister and that of the ordained. The texts of the rites included in this book are specifically for lay ministers.

THE GOSPELS FOR SUNDAYS AND HOLY DAYS OF OBLIGATION

Following the rites are the Gospel readings for Sundays and holy days of obligation for Year C. (Remember, the Church is on a three-year cycle of readings. For 2007 the readings for Year C are used. In 2008 the readings are from Year A.) The Church recommends reading the week's Sunday Gospel during the Communion rite as one important way of uniting the communicants in spirit with the parish from which sickness or age has separated them.

In this book, the Gospels are clearly organized by date and the title of particular celebrations so that you can easily find the appropriate reading. For example, if you make your visit during the Second Week of Ordinary Time, you will use the Gospel for the Second Sunday of Ordinary Time. In 2007, this Sunday of Ordinary Time is January 14. Simply look for that date and the title of the celebration and you will know which Gospel to use. These are also indicated in the Table of Contents of this book. For some celebrations, such as Palm Sunday, the Lectionary provides a longer and shorter form for the Gospel. For simplicity, only the short form is included in this resource.

If you are visiting on a holy day of obligation, use the Gospels prescribed for these days. You can also locate these Gospels by date and title. In the dioceses of the United States of America, the holy days of obligation occurring in 2007 (Year C) are

- Solemnity of the Immaculate Conception of the Blessed Virgin Mary (December 8, 2006)

- Solemnity of the Nativity of the Lord (December 25, 2007)

- Solemnity of the Ascension of the Lord (May 17 or May 20, 2007)

- Solemnity of the Assumption of the Blessed Virgin Mary (August 15, 2007)
- Solemnity of All Saints (November 1, 2007)

"Regarding the Ascension of the Lord, the ecclesiastical Provinces of Boston, Hartford, New York, Newark, Philadelphia, and the state of Nebraska have retained its proper celebration on the proper Thursday. In these Provinces, the readings for the day are from the solemnity of the Ascension of the Lord. In all other Provinces that have transferred this solemnity to the Seventh Sunday of Easter, on that day (7th Sunday of Easter), the readings are from the Ascension of the Lord" (*Ordo,* Paulist Press).

EXPLANATION OF THE READINGS

You will notice that the rite offers an opportunity for the Extraordinary Minister of Holy Communion to give a brief explanation of the reading with special reference to the experience of the sick or aging person and the caregivers. You might want to base your explanation and reflection on the parish Sunday homily in order to deepen the sense of connection you are trying encourage. If you feel uncomfortable about speaking, it's better either to say just an informal sentence or two or to say nothing than to read a homily or commentary from a book. The word of God itself creates a bond between reader and hearers, breaking down the sense of isolation that afflicts sufferers. Words written by a stranger are too impersonal to support this pastoral relationship.

PATRON SAINTS

Finally, there is a list of saints whom the Church has identified as particular intercessors, companions, and guides for those suffering from various kinds of ailments. If you feel that the sick or aging person might welcome the company and support of a saint, you might want to include the saint's name in the intercessions and suggest that those you are visiting continue to ask for the saint's help. An example of an intercession would be: "For all those who suffer from throat cancer, especially N. (insert the name of the person or persons present), that through the intercession of Saint Blaise, may find comfort and strength, we pray to the Lord." This book does not provide any information about the saints listed, but there are many books and websites where you can find their stories. Such resources are Butler's *Lives of the Saints* (published by the Liturgical Press) and Catholic Online (www.catholic.org/saints/).

BEYOND THE BOOK

The official rites offer appropriate prayers and clear directions, but they don't tell you everything you need to know in order to celebrate the Communion rite effectively. Here are some practical hints that may help.

GETTING FROM THE PARISH CHURCH TO THE SICK ROOM

Scheduling a Communion Visit: Some parishes assign ministers to visit particular people but encourage them to make their own arrangements regarding the day and time. Both the sick and their caregivers, at home or in institutional facilities, appreciate being able to negotiate appropriate times for Communion. You don't want to drop in when patients are absent from their rooms for tests or treatments, for example.

If you are asked to take Communion at times other than during Sunday Mass, please make sure your training includes information about where to find the tabernacle key and how to approach the tabernacle reverently, open it, and transfer the hosts you will need from the ciborium in which they are kept, to the container you will use to carry the Blessed Sacrament to the sick (see below). Ordinarily, you would pray briefly before the tabernacle, purify your fingers in a small vessel of water that is usually kept beside the tabernacle for that purpose, wipe them on a finger towel also usually kept there, and genuflect after opening the tabernacle. If your parish does not provide either the small vessel or a finger towel, purify your fingers as best as you are able. While you are carrying the Blessed Sacrament, remember that Christ is with you and for what purpose. You will find some suggestions about appropriate reverence below. If you have unused hosts left over at the end of your rounds, you must bring them back to the parish church and replace them in the tabernacle. After closing the tabernacle, you again purify your fingers. If you wish to avoid having hosts that must be returned, you can give the last few communicants more than one host so that all the hosts are consumed. However, you may not simply consume them yourself after your last visit or take them home to return later to the church.

Bringing What You Need: Make a checklist of what you want to have with you before you leave home. You'll find some suggestions below. Don't forget this book! It does happen. But if it does, don't panic, and don't fail to keep your appointment. As a precaution, memorize the outline of the rite or keep a copy of a simple outline in your pocket, wallet, or purse. In this case, do make up your own prayer, but keep it very short and simple. Borrow a Bible or summarize the Gospel in your own words. God works through all our weaknesses and mistakes.

Carrying the Blessed Sacrament: The Blessed Sacrament is carried in a small box called a *pyx* or in another dignified container reserved exclusively for that purpose. Some pyxes can be worn on a cord around the neck. Your parish will probably supply you with what you need. When you are carrying the Blessed Sacrament, try to remember and attend reverently and prayerfully to Christ present, choosing your activities appropriately, without becoming artificially silent or stilted in your conversation, especially with those who are not aware of what you are carrying or of its significance. On the one hand, avoid distractions such as loud music, "talk" programs or tapes, or other things that would disturb prayer while you are en route. On the other hand, while avoiding such distractions, be careful not to be rude to people who greet you or speak to you in passing as you walk to your destination. Christ is not offended by the company and conversation of human beings!

PREPARING AN ENVIRONMENT FOR PRAYER
ENCOUNTERING CHRIST IN PERSONS

The medical world can be very impersonal. Church ministry is not. It is important that you spend a few minutes at the beginning of your visit to get to know those present and give them a chance to feel comfortable with you. Your parish may be able to supply you with helpful information in advance of your visit. In return, it would be useful to other Extraordinary Ministers of Holy Communion if you were to report back what you had learned about the condition, circumstances, and needs of those you visit.

When you arrive, put those present at ease by engaging in a few moments of personal conversation. Tell them your name and remind them that the parish has sent you. Ask them how they are and listen attentively to their answers. Show your interest and concern, but remember that you are not there to offer medical advice or to pass judgment on medical matters, even if you yourself are a professional medical caregiver. If you can, address the sick or aging person and the main caregivers by name, but be aware that not everyone likes to be addressed by a first name without permission. Sickness or debilitating aging often rob people of their sense of personal dignity, so treating people with respect is an important dimension of your ministry. Whatever their condition, you and they are both collaborators in Christ's work. Ministry is a two-way street: those whom you visit are serving you by their witness to Christ suffering as much as you are serving them by offering them Christ in Communion. Take note of any special needs you see: Is the sick or aging person low on energy, in pain, limited in motion, hard of hearing? You will want to tailor the length, content, and style of the celebration accordingly.

CREATING AN ENVIRONMENT FOR PRAYER

PREPARING YOURSELF TO LEAD PRAYER

The world of the sick and aging confined to home or, especially, to a hospital or geriatric facility may not feel much like a place of prayer. The most important element in creating an environment for prayer is you. The minister who prays while leading others in prayer is the most powerful invitation one can offer to those who need to be called from all the preoccupations of suffering into deeper awareness of the mystery of God present and acting in our midst.

Here are some steps you can take to develop this important skill:

1. Devote praying, reading, and meditating on the texts of the prayers and readings provided in this book. You will best pray them in public if you have already prayed them many times in private.

2. Familiarize yourself thoroughly with the structure and flow of the rites so that you can concentrate on the people rather than the book. You need not memorize prayers or readings. Simply know what comes next and where to find it.

3. Before you go into the building or sick room, pray briefly, asking Christ to work through you; after the visit, pause to give thanks.

4. Reflect on your experience after you return home. Were there moments during the celebration when you felt uncertain or distracted? Why? What could you do next time to make yourself more at ease so that you can pray more attentively without losing contact with those you are leading in prayer? Sharing your experiences with other Extraordinary Ministers of Holy Communion and/or parish staff can be a useful way to continue and deepen everyone's ongoing ministry formation.

PREPARING THE ROOM FOR PRAYER

You can also take some simple steps to establish an atmosphere that encourages prayer. Take a small white cloth and a candle with you to prepare a place on which to put the pyx containing the Blessed Sacrament as a focus for the celebration. (Be sure you have something with which to light the candle!) Caregivers familiar with the rite may have prepared a place in advance, but many will not. A small standing crucifix, cross, or icon heightens consciousness of Christ.

Be aware of the restrictions you may face in a health care or geriatric facility. The rite recommends that the minister be accompanied by a candlebearer and place a candle on the table where the Blessed Sacrament will stand during the celebration, as described above. However, safety regulations usually forbid the use of open flames in institutions. Oxygen and other substances that might be in use are highly flammable. Moreover, you may not be able to find any appropriate surface other than a bedside table or nightstand that will have to be cleared before you can set up a place for the Blessed Sacrament. Be prepared to make whatever practical adjustments the circumstances require. If you've never visited a particular hospital unit or nursing home, see if you can find another minister who has and find out what to expect.

PREPARING PARTICIPANTS FOR PRAYER

After a few moments of conversation, find a graceful way to end the social part of the visit without seeming disinterested or abrupt. Then give the participants a simple, brief overview of the Communion rite so they will know what to expect, unless you know they are already familiar with it. Surprises tend to disrupt prayer! Finally, mark the beginning of prayer clearly by inviting silent attentiveness, making the sign of the cross and moving into the service itself.

RECOGNIZING THE RECIPIENT

WHO MAY RECEIVE COMMUNION?

Catholic shut-ins, caregivers, or others who assemble with them may receive Communion, provided the usual conditions have been met. You can offer that invitation before you begin the Communion rite, being careful not to embarrass or offend those who are not able to receive. "The elderly, the infirm, and those who care for them can receive the Most Holy Eucharist even if they have eaten something within the preceding hour" (Code of Canon Law, 919§3).

SPECIAL CIRCUMSTANCES

Unfortunately, neither sickness nor the deterioration sometimes brought on by aging is neat or predictable. The physical, psychological, and spiritual condition of those you visit may have changed since the arrangements for Communion were made.

Sometimes those you are visiting will express reluctance to receive. They may or may not want to tell you why. They might be embarrassed to say that they are too nauseated; they might feel alienated from God; they might need sacramental absolution but don't want to say so. You are obviously a person of generosity and compassion, or you wouldn't have volunteered to be a Communion minister. However, a Communion visit is not the best time to identify and try to resolve serious personal and/or spiritual problems. Be aware of your status and of the vulnerability of the suffering: you represent the Church, and you have more power than you may realize to make others feel guilty by showing that you disapprove of their decision not to receive Communion or by giving the impression that they have "wasted" your time. Remember that they are not rejecting you as a person. Rather, they are struggling with something deeper. Offer to pray with them, using whatever texts of the rite seem appropriate and inviting them to enter more deeply into communion with the suffering and risen Christ who loves them. Let them know what pastoral resources are available to them: offer to return or to send another minister at a more convenient time; provide the parish phone number; offer to let the pastoral staff know that they would like a priest to visit, without forcing them to reply.

Sometimes you may find that those you are visiting are unable to swallow easily. Consult medical caregivers. If they give permission, you may break the host into the smallest of pieces, place a piece on the person's tongue to dissolve, and follow with a glass of water to make swallowing possible.

You may even find that someone cannot ingest the host at all. In such cases, the person may receive the Blood of Christ instead, but that requires specialized vessels and procedures. Report the circumstances to your pastor, or to the professional pastoral care parish staff if the person is in a health care or geriatric facility. They will be able to give Communion appropriately. In the meantime, pray with those you are visiting, read and explain the Gospel if they are able to follow, and offer them the support of your presence and prayer.

Any of the seriously ill, but especially hospice patients, may move more quickly than expected toward death. A person who faces death within days should receive Communion under the form of Viaticum. *Viaticum* means something like "travel with you," but it is often translated as food for the journey. The Eucharist as Viaticum is the sacrament which, with Anointing and Penance, prepares a person for the final journey. Catholics are seriously obligated to receive Viaticum if at all possible. The time for using the special comforting and strengthening prayers of the rite of Viaticum to administer Communion is while the person is still conscious and able to swallow. Once death has become imminent, dying persons may receive Viaticum every day for as long as they are able. An Extraordinary Minister of Holy Communion may and should give Viaticum, but the necessary texts are not found in this particular book because they will rarely be needed by a minister bringing Communion from Sunday Mass for shut-ins whose condition is known to the parish staff. The dying will usually receive a Communion visit from someone who is prepared in advance to administer Viaticum. If someone you are visiting is clearly dying, please notify your parish staff, but don't hesitate to give Communion if the person can swallow, as well as making sure the person has the opportunity for Penance and Annointing if he or she desires.

Also, be aware that the hospitalized may not be permitted to take anything by mouth for a period of time prior to certain tests or treatments. Even a small piece of the host received at such times may cause medical personnel to cancel the planned procedure. If you see a sign that says, "NPO," initials for the

Latin phrase meaning "nothing by mouth," ask a member of the medical staff if you may administer Communion, but expect a "no." In this case, too, you should still pray with the sick or aging, read the Gospel and explain it, and offer the comfort of Christ's presence through your own and that of the parish you represent.

It is important that the Extraordinary Minister of Holy Communion keeps in mind the sacramental rites which are an essential part of the Church's ministry to the sick and dying and which can be administered only by an ordained priest—the sacraments of Penance or Reconciliation and the Anointing of the Sick. As appropriate, it is part of your ministry to bring these to the attention of the sick and those confined to their homes and, if need be, help them contact a priest.

It's best to familiarize yourself with the rites the Church provides for circumstances where the person(s) are not able to receive Communion. These rites are found in the *Pastoral Care of the Sick:* Visits to the Sick and Visits to a Sick Child, as well as the *Book of Blessings:* Orders for the Blessing of the Sick.

THE TABLE SET, THE TABLE SHARED

Among these nuts and bolts of lay Communion ministry, never lose sight of your purpose. You have been commissioned to serve at the Good Shepherd's table, set before the sick and aging in face of our common enemies, suffering and mortality. With your parish or diocesan training program, the support of your parish pastoral staff and other Extraordinary Ministers of Holy Communion, this book, and your growing experience, you have many of the tools you will need. However, the most important tool is one that only Christ can provide for you. The more deeply you yourself enter into the Communion of the table, the more clearly you will see that sick and healthy, young and old, newborn and dying, we are all one Body. In that Body, we are *all* servants at the table we share, building one another up in faith and love until that day when, by God's gracious gift, we will all dwell together in the Lord's own house for ever and ever.

LTP appreciates your comments and suggestions. Please e-mail the editorial team at CHVS@ltp.org.

Genevieve Glen, OSB
Abbey of Saint Walburga
Virginia Dale, Colorado
October 2005

Sister Genevieve Glen, OSB, is a Benedictine nun of the contemplative Abbey of St. Walburga in Virginia Dale, Colorado. She holds master's degrees in systematic theology from Saint John's University, Collegeville, Minnesota, and in spirituality from The Catholic University of America in Washington, DC, where she also did extensive doctoral studies in liturgy. She has lectured and written extensively on the Church's rites for the sick and dying. She is co-author of the *Handbook for Ministers of Care*, second edition (Liturgy Training Publications) and contributing editor of *Recovering the Riches of Anointing: A Study of the Sacrament of the Sick* (The Liturgical Press).

THE RITES

INTRODUCTION

Whoever eats this bread will live for ever.

71.   This chapter contains two rites: one for use when communion can be celebrated in the context of a liturgy of the word; the other, a brief communion rite for use in more restrictive circumstances, such as in hospitals.

72.   Priests with pastoral responsibilities should see to it that the sick or aged, even though not seriously ill or in danger of death, are given every opportunity to receive the eucharist frequently, even daily, especially during the Easter season. They may receive communion at any hour. Those who care for the sick may receive communion with them, in accord with the usual norms. To provide frequent communion for the sick, it may be necessary to ensure that the community has a sufficient number of ministers of communion. The communion minister should wear attire appropriate to this ministry.

The sick person and others may help to plan the celebration, for example, by choosing the prayers and readings. Those making these choices should keep in mind the condition of the sick person. The readings and the homily should help those present to reach a deeper understanding of the mystery of human suffering in relation to the paschal mystery of Christ.

73.   The faithful who are ill are deprived of their rightful and accustomed place in the eucharistic community. In bringing communion to them the minister of communion represents Christ and manifests faith and charity on behalf of the whole community toward those who cannot be present at the eucharist. For the sick the reception of communion is not only a privilege but also a sign

of support and concern shown by the Christian community for its members who are ill.

The links between the community's eucharistic celebration, especially on the Lord's Day, and the communion of the sick are intimate and manifold. Besides remembering the sick in the general intercessions at Mass, those present should be reminded occasionally of the significance of communion in the lives of those who are ill: union with Christ in his struggle with evil, his prayer for the world, and his love for the Father, and union with the community from which they are separated.

The obligation to visit and comfort those who cannot take part in the eucharistic assembly may be clearly demonstrated by taking communion to them from the community's eucharistic celebration. This symbol of unity between the community and its sick members has the deepest significance on the Lord's Day, the special day of the eucharistic assembly.

74.   When the eucharist is brought to the sick, it should be carried in a pyx or small closed container. Those who are with the sick should be asked to prepare a table covered with a linen cloth upon which the blessed sacrament will be placed. Lighted candles are prepared and, where it is customary, a vessel of holy water. Care should be taken to make the occasion special and joyful.

Sick people who are unable to receive communion under the form of bread may receive it under the form of wine alone. If the wine is consecrated at a Mass not celebrated in the presence of the sick person, the blood of the Lord is kept in a properly covered vessel and is placed in the tabernacle after communion. The precious blood should be carried to the sick in a vessel which is closed in such a way as to eliminate all danger of spilling. If some of the precious blood remains, it should be consumed by the minister, who should also see to it that the vessel is properly purified.

75.   If the sick wish to celebrate the sacrament of penance, it is preferable that the priest make himself available for this during a previous visit.

76.   If it is necessary to celebrate the sacrament of penance during the rite of communion, it takes the place of the penitential rite.

COMMUNION IN ORDINARY CIRCUMSTANCES

77.   If possible, provision should be made to celebrate Mass in the homes of the sick, with their families and friends gathered around them. The Ordinary determines the conditions and requirements for such celebrations.

COMMUNION IN A HOSPITAL OR INSTITUTION

78.   There will be situations, particularly in large institutions with many communicants, when the minister should consider alternative means so that the rite of communion of the sick is not diminished to the absolute minimum. In such cases the following alternatives should be considered: (a) where possible, the residents or patients may be gathered in groups in one or more areas; (b) additional ministers of communion may assist.

When it is not possible to celebrate the full rite, the rite for communion in a hospital or institution may be used. If it is convenient, however, the minister may add elements from the rite for ordinary circumstances, for example, a Scripture reading.

79.   The rite begins with the recitation of the eucharistic antiphon in the church, the hospital chapel, or the first room visited. Then the minister gives communion to the sick in their individual rooms.

80.   The concluding prayer may be said in the church, the hospital chapel, or the last room visited. No blessing is given.

COMMUNION IN
ORDINARY CIRCUMSTANCES

OUTLINE OF THE RITE

Introductory Rites
    Greeting
    Penitential Rite
Liturgy of the Word
    Reading
    Response
    General Intercessions
Liturgy of Holy Communion
    The Lord's Prayer
    Communion
    Silent Prayer
    Prayer after Communion
Concluding Rite
    Blessing

COMMUNION IN ORDINARY CIRCUMSTANCES

INTRODUCTORY RITES

Greeting

81. *The minister greets the sick person and the others present. One of the following may be used:*

A

The peace of the Lord be with you always.

R. *And also with you.*

B

Peace be with you (this house) and with all who live here.

R. And also with you.

C

The grace of our Lord Jesus Christ and the love of God and the fellowship of the Holy Spirit be with you all.

R. And also with you.

D

The grace and peace of God our Father and the Lord Jesus Christ be with you.

R. And also with you.

The minister then places the blessed sacrament on the table, and all join in adoration.

Penitential Rite

83. The minister invites the sick person and all present to join in the penitential rite, using these or similar words:

A

My brothers and sisters, to prepare ourselves for this celebration, let us call to mind our sins.

B

My brothers and sisters, let us turn with confidence to
the Lord and ask his forgiveness for all our sins.

*After a brief period of silence, the penitential rite continues, using
one of the following:*

A

Lord Jesus, you healed the sick:
Lord, have mercy.

R. *Lord, have mercy.*

Lord Jesus, you forgave sinners:
Christ, have mercy.

R. *Christ, have mercy.*

Lord Jesus, you give us yourself to heal us
    and bring us strength:
Lord, have mercy.

R. *Lord, have mercy.*

B

All say:

I confess to almighty God,
and to you, my brothers and sisters,
that I have sinned through my own fault

They strike their breast.

in my thoughts and in my words,
in what I have done,
and in what I have failed to do;
and I ask blessed Mary, ever virgin,
all the angels and saints,
and you, my brothers and sisters,
to pray for me to the Lord our God.

The minister concludes the penitential rite with the following:

May almighty God have mercy on us,
forgive us our sins,
and bring us to everlasting life.

R. Amen.

LITURGY OF THE WORD
Reading

84. *The word of God is proclaimed by one of those present or by the minister.*

[The Gospels for Sundays and Holy Days of Obligation are found on pages 38–128. Use the Gospel for the appropriate date of celebration.]

Response

85. *A brief period of silence may be observed after the reading of the word of God.*

The minister may then give a brief explanation of the reading, applying it to the needs of the sick person and those who are looking after him or her.

General Intercessions

86. The general intercessions may be said. With a brief introduction the minister invites all those present to pray. After the intentions the minister says the concluding prayer. It is desirable that the intentions be announced by someone other than the minister.

LITURGY OF HOLY COMMUNION
The Lord's Prayer

87. The minister introduces the Lord's Prayer in these or similar words:

A

Now let us pray as Christ the Lord has taught us:

B

And now let us pray with confidence as Christ our Lord commanded:

All say:

Our Father,
who art in heaven,
hallowed be thy name;

thy kingdom come;
thy will be done on earth as it is in heaven.
Give us this day, our daily bread;
and forgive us our trespasses
as we forgive those who trespass against us;
and lead us not into temptation,
but deliver us from evil. Amen.

Communion

88. The minister shows the eucharistic bread to those present, saying:

A
This is the bread of life.
Taste and see that the Lord is good.

B
This is the Lamb of God
who takes away the sins of the world.
Happy are those who are called to his supper.

The sick person and all who are to receive communion say:

Lord, I am not worthy to receive you,
but only say the word and I shall be healed.

The minister goes to the sick person and, showing the blessed sacrament, says:

The body of Christ.

The sick person answers: "Amen," and receives communion.

Then the minister says:

The blood of Christ.

The sick person answers: "Amen," and receives communion.

Others present who wish to receive communion then do so in the usual way.

After the conclusion of the rite, the minister cleanses the vessel as usual.

Silent Prayer

89. *Then a period of silence may be observed.*

Prayer after Communion

90. *The minister says a concluding prayer. One of the following may be used:*

Let us pray.

Pause for silent prayer, if this has not preceded.

A
God our Father,
you have called us to share the one bread and one cup
and so become one in Christ.

Help us to live in him
that we may bear fruit,
rejoicing that he has redeemed the world.

We ask this through Christ our Lord.

R. Amen.

B
All-powerful God,
we thank you for the nourishment you give us
through your holy gift.

Pour out your Spirit upon us
and in the strength of this food from heaven
keep us single-minded in your service.

We ask this in the name of Jesus the Lord.

R. Amen.

C
All-powerful and ever-living God,
may the body and blood of Christ your Son
be for our brother/sister N.
a lasting remedy for body and soul.

We ask this through Christ our Lord.

R. Amen.

CONCLUDING RITE

Blessing

91. A minister who is not a priest or deacon invokes God's blessing and makes the sign of the cross on himself or herself, while saying:

A

May the Lord bless us,
protect us from all evil,
and bring us to everlasting life.

R. Amen.

B

May the almighty and merciful God bless and protect us,
the Father, and the Son, ✚ and the Holy Spirit.

R. Amen.

Communion in a Hospital or Institution

OUTLINE OF THE RITE

Introductory Rite
    Antiphon
Liturgy of Holy Communion
    Greeting
    The Lord's Prayer
    Communion
Concluding Rite
    Concluding Prayer

COMMUNION IN A HOSPITAL OR INSTITUTION

INTRODUCTORY RITE

Antiphon

92. *The rite may begin in the church, the hospital chapel, or the first room, where the minister says one of the following antiphons:*

A

How holy this feast
in which Christ is our food:
his passion is recalled;
grace fills our hearts;
and we receive a pledge of the glory to come.

B

How gracious you are, Lord:
your gift of bread from heaven
reveals a Father's love and brings us perfect joy.
You fill the hungry with good things
and send the rich away empty.

C

I am the living bread
come down from heaven.
If you eat this bread
you will live for ever.
The bread I will give is my flesh
for the life of the world.

If it is customary, the minister may be accompanied by a person carrying a candle.

LITURGY OF HOLY COMMUNION

Greeting

93. On entering each room, the minister may use one of the following greetings:

A

The peace of the Lord be with you always.

R. *And also with you.*

B

The grace of our Lord Jesus Christ and the love of God and the fellowship of the Holy Spirit be with you all.

R. And also with you.

The minister then places the blessed sacrament on the table, and all join in adoration.

If there is time and it seems desirable, the minister may proclaim a scripture reading.

The Lord's Prayer

94. *When circumstances permit (for example, when there are not many rooms to visit), the minister is encouraged to lead the sick in the Lord's Prayer. The minister introduces the Lord's Prayer in these or similar words:*

A

Jesus taught us to call God our Father, and so we have the courage to say:

B

Now let us pray as Christ the Lord has taught us:

All say:

Our Father,
who art in heaven,
hallowed be thy name;
thy kingdom come;

thy will be done on earth as it is in heaven.
Give us this day, our daily bread;
and forgive us our trespasses
as we forgive those who trespass against us;
and lead us not into temptation,
but deliver us from evil. Amen.

Communion

95. *The minister shows the eucharistic bread to those present,*
saying:

A

This is the Lamb of God
who takes away the sins of the world.
Happy are those who hunger and thirst,
for they shall be satisfied.

B

This it the bread of life,
Taste and see that the Lord is good.

The sick person and all who are to receive communion say:

Lord, I am not worthy to receive you,
but only say the word and I shall be healed.

The minister goes to the sick person and, showing the blessed
sacrament, says:

The body of Christ.

The sick person answers: "Amen," and receives communion.

Then the minister says:

The blood of Christ.

The sick person answers: "Amen," and receives communion.

Others present who wish to receive communion then do so in the usual way.

CONCLUDING RITE
Concluding Prayer

96. The concluding prayer may be said either in the last room visited, in the church, or chapel. One of the following may be used:

Let us pray.

Pause for silent prayer.

A

God our Father,
you have called us to share the one bread and one cup
and so become one in Christ.

Help us to live in him
that we may bear fruit,
rejoicing that he has redeemed the world.

We ask this through Christ our Lord.

R. Amen.

B

All-powerful and ever-living God,
may the body and blood of Christ your Son
be for our brothers and sisters
a lasting remedy for body and soul.

We ask this through Christ our Lord.

R. Amen.

C

All-powerful God,
we thank you for the nourishment you give us
through your holy gift.

Pour out your Spirit upon us
and in the strength of this food from heaven
keep us single-minded in your service.

We ask this in the name of Jesus the Lord.

R. Amen.

The blessing is omitted and the minister cleanses the vessel as usual.

THE GOSPELS FOR SUNDAYS AND HOLY DAYS OF OBLIGATION

The Gospels for Sundays and Holy Days of Obligation

December 3, 2006

First Sunday of Advent

Your redemption is at hand.

A reading from the holy Gospel according to Luke
21:25–28, 34–36

Jesus said to his disciples:
"There will be signs in the sun, the moon and the stars,
   and on earth nations will be in dismay,
   perplexed by the roaring of the sea and the waves.
People will die of fright
   in anticipation of what is coming upon the world,
   for the powers of the heavens will be shaken.
And then they will see the Son of Man
   coming in a cloud with power and great glory.
But when these signs begin to happen,
   stand erect and raise your heads
   because your redemption is at hand.

"Beware that your hearts do not become drowsy
   from carousing and drunkenness
   and the anxieties of daily life,
   and that day catch you by surprise like a trap.

For that day will assault everyone
   who lives on the face of the earth.
Be vigilant at all times
   and pray that you have the strength
   to escape the tribulations that are imminent
   and to stand before the Son of Man."

The Gospel of the Lord.

December 8, 2006

THE IMMACULATE CONCEPTION OF THE BLESSED VIRGIN MARY

Hail, full of grace! The Lord is with you.

A reading from the holy Gospel according to Luke   *1:26–38*

The angel Gabriel was sent from God
   to a town of Galilee called Nazareth,
   to a virgin betrothed to a man named Joseph,
   of the house of David,
   and the virgin's name was Mary.
And coming to her, he said,
   "Hail, full of grace! The Lord is with you."
But she was greatly troubled at what was said
   and pondered what sort of greeting this might be.

Then the angel said to her,
  "Do not be afraid, Mary,
  for you have found favor with God.
Behold, you will conceive in your womb and bear a son,
  and you shall name him Jesus.
He will be great and will be called Son of the Most High,
  and the Lord God will give him the throne of David
    his father,
  and he will rule over the house of Jacob forever,
  and of his Kingdom there will be no end."
But Mary said to the angel,
  "How can this be,
  since I have no relations with a man?"
And the angel said to her in reply,
  "The Holy Spirit will come upon you,
  and the power of the Most High will overshadow you.
Therefore the child to be born
  will be called holy, the Son of God.
And behold, Elizabeth, your relative,
  has also concieved a son in her old age,
  and this is the sixth month for her who was
    called barren;
  for nothing will be impossible for God."
Mary said, "Behold, I am the handmaid of the Lord.
May it be done to me according to your word."
Then the angel departed from her.

The Gospel of the Lord.

December 10, 2006

Second Sunday of Advent

All flesh shall see the salvation of God.

A reading from the holy Gospel according to Luke

3:1–6

In the fifteenth year of the reign of Tiberius Caesar,
   when Pontius Pilate was governor of Judea,
   and Herod was tetrarch of Galilee,
   and his brother Philip tetrarch of the region
      of Ituraea and Trachonitis,
   and Lysanias was tetrarch of Abilene,
   during the high priesthood of Annas and Caiaphas,
   the word of God came to John the son of Zechariah
      in the desert.
John went throughout the whole region of the Jordan,
   proclaiming a baptism of repentance for the
      forgiveness of sins,
   as it is written in the book of the words of the
      prophet Isaiah:
   A voice of one crying out in the desert:
   "Prepare the way of the Lord,
      make straight his paths.
   Every valley shall be filled
      and every mountain and hill shall be made low.

> *The winding roads shall be made straight,*
> *and the rough ways made smooth,*
> *and all flesh shall see the salvation of God."*

The Gospel of the Lord.

December 17, 2006

THIRD SUNDAY OF ADVENT

What should we do?

A reading from the holy Gospel according to Luke
3:10–18

The crowds asked John the Baptist,
  "What should we do?"
He said to them in reply,
  "Whoever has two cloaks
should share with the person who has none.
And whoever has food should do likewise."
Even tax collectors came to be baptized and they said
    to him,
  "Teacher, what should we do?"
He answered them,
  "Stop collecting more than what is prescribed."
Soldiers also asked him,
  "And what is it that we should do?"

He told them,
  "Do not practice extortion,
  do not falsely accuse anyone,
  and be satisfied with your wages."

Now the people were filled with expectation,
  and all were asking in their hearts
  whether John might be the Christ.
John answered them all, saying,
  "I am baptizing you with water,
  but one mightier than I is coming.
I am not worthy to loosen the thongs of his sandals.
He will baptize you with the Holy Spirit and fire.
His winnowing fan is in his hand to clear his
     threshing floor
  and to gather the wheat into his barn,
  but the chaff he will burn with unquenchable fire."
Exhorting them in many other ways,
  he preached good news to the people.

The Gospel of the Lord.

December 24, 2006

FOURTH SUNDAY OF ADVENT

And how does this happen to me, that the mother of my Lord should come to me?

A reading from the holy Gospel according to Luke

1:39–45

Mary set out
  and traveled to the hill country in haste
  to a town of Judah,
  where she entered the house of Zechariah
  and greeted Elizabeth.
When Elizabeth heard Mary's greeting,
  the infant leaped in her womb,
  and Elizabeth, filled with the Holy Spirit,
  cried out in a loud voice and said,
  "Blessed are you among women,
  and blessed is the fruit of your womb.
And how does this happen to me,
  that the mother of my Lord should come to me?
For at the moment the sound of your greeting reached
      my ears,
  the infant in my womb leaped for joy.
Blessed are you who believed
  that what was spoken to you by the Lord
  would be fulfilled."

The Gospel of the Lord.

December 25, 2006

THE NATIVITY OF THE LORD

Today a savior has been born for you.

A reading from the holy Gospel according to Luke 2:1–14

In those days a decree went out from Caesar Augustus
   that the whole world should be enrolled.
This was the first enrollment,
   when Quirinius was governor of Syria.
So all went to be enrolled, each to his own town.
And Joseph too went up from Galilee from the town
    of Nazareth
   to Judea, to the city of David that is called Bethlehem,
   because he was of the house and family of David,
   to be enrolled with Mary, his betrothed, who was
    with child.
While they were there,
   the time came for her to have her child,
   and she gave birth to her firstborn son.
She wrapped him in swaddling clothes and laid him in
    a manger,
   because there was no room for them in the inn.

Now there were shepherds in that region living in
    the fields
   and keeping the night watch over their flock.

The angel of the Lord appeared to them
    and the glory of the Lord shone around them,
    and they were struck with great fear.
The angel said to them,
    "Do not be afraid;
    for behold, I proclaim to you good news of great joy
    that will be for all the people.
For today in the city of David
    a savior has been born for you who is Christ and Lord.
And this will be a sign for you:
    you will find an infant wrapped in swaddling clothes
    and lying in a manger."
And suddenly there was a multitude of the heavenly host
        with the angel,
    praising God and saying:
        "Glory to God in the highest
            and on earth peace to those on whom his
                favor rests."

The Gospel of the Lord.

Mass at Midnight

December 31, 2006

The Holy Family of Jesus, Mary, and Joseph

His parents found Jesus sitting in the midst of the teachers.

A reading from the holy Gospel according to Luke
2:41–52

Each year Jesus' parents went to Jerusalem for the feast
    of Passover,
    and when he was twelve years old,
    they went up according to festival custom.
After they had completed its days, as they were
    returning,
    the boy Jesus remained behind in Jerusalem,
    but his parents did not know it.
Thinking that he was in the caravan,
    they journeyed for a day
    and looked for him among their relatives and
      acquaintances,
    but not finding him,
    they returned to Jerusalem to look for him.
After three days they found him in the temple,
    sitting in the midst of the teachers,
    listening to them and asking them questions,
    and all who heard him were astounded
    at his understanding and his answers.
When his parents saw him,
    they were astonished,

and his mother said to him,
  "Son, why have you done this to us?
Your father and I have been looking for you with
    great anxiety."
And he said to them,
  "Why were you looking for me?
Did you not know that I must be in my Father's house?"
But they did not understand what he said to them.
He went down with them and came to Nazareth,
  and was obedient to them;
  and his mother kept all these things in her heart.
And Jesus advanced in wisdom and age and favor
  before God and man.

The Gospel of the Lord.

January 7, 2007

THE EPIPHANY OF THE LORD

We saw his start at its rising and have come to do him homage.

A reading from the holy Gospel according to Matthew

2:1–12

When Jesus was born in Bethlehem of Judea,
  in the days of King Herod,
  behold, magi from the east arrived in Jerusalem,
    saying,
  "Where is the newborn king of the Jews?

We saw his star at its rising
and have come to do him homage."
When King Herod heard this,
he was greatly troubled,
and all Jerusalem with him.
Assembling all the chief priests and the scribes of
the people,
he inquired of them where the Christ was to be born.
They said to him, "In Bethlehem of Judea,
for thus it has been written through the prophet:
And you, Bethlehem, land of Judah,
are by no means least among the rulers of Judah;
since from you shall come a ruler,
who is to shepherd my people Israel."
Then Herod called the magi secretly
and ascertained from them the time of the
star's appearance.
He sent them to Bethlehem and said,
"Go and search diligently for the child.
When you have found him, bring me word,
that I too may go and do him homage."
After their audience with the king they set out.
And behold, the star that they had seen at its rising
preceded them,
until it came and stopped over the place where the
child was.
They were overjoyed at seeing the star,
and on entering the house
they saw the child with Mary his mother.

They prostrated themselves and did him homage.
Then they opened their treasures
  and offered him gifts of gold, frankincense, and myrrh.
And having been warned in a dream not to return
    to Herod,
  they departed for their country by another way.

The Gospel of the Lord.

January 14, 2007

SECOND SUNDAY IN ORDINARY TIME

Jesus did this as the beginning of his signs at Cana in Galilee.

A reading from the holy Gospel according to John

2:1–11

There was a wedding at Cana in Galilee,
  and the mother of Jesus was there.
Jesus and his disciples were also invited to the wedding.
When the wine ran short,
  the mother of Jesus said to him,
  "They have no wine."
And Jesus said to her,
  "Woman, how does your concern affect me?
My hour has not yet come."
His mother said to the servers,
  "Do whatever he tells you."

Now there were six stone water jars there for Jewish
    ceremonial washings,
  each holding twenty to thirty gallons.
Jesus told them,
  "Fill the jars with water."
So they filled them to the brim.
Then he told them,
  "Draw some out now and take it to the headwaiter."
So they took it.
And when the headwaiter tasted the water that had
    become wine,
  without knowing where it came from
  —although the servers who had drawn the
    water knew—,
  the headwaiter called the bridegroom and said to him,
  "Everyone serves good wine first,
  and then when people have drunk freely, an
    inferior one;
  but you have kept the good wine until now."
Jesus did this as the beginning of his signs at Cana
    in Galilee
  and so revealed his glory,
  and his disciples began to believe in him.

The Gospel of the Lord.

January 21, 2007

THIRD SUNDAY IN ORDINARY TIME

Today this Scripture passage is fulfilled.

A reading from the holy Gospel according to Luke

1:1–4; 4:14–21

Since many have undertaken to compile a narrative of
    the events
  that have been fulfilled among us,
  just as those who were eyewitnesses from
    the beginning
  and ministers of the word have handed them down
    to us,
  I too have decided,
  after investigating everything accurately anew,
  to write it down in an orderly sequence for you,
  most excellent Theophilus,
  so that you may realize the certainty of the teachings
  you have received.

Jesus returned to Galilee in the power of the Spirit,
  and news of him spread throughout the whole region.
He taught in their synagogues and was praised by all.

He came to Nazareth, where he had grown up,
  and went according to his custom
  into the synagogue on the sabbath day.
He stood up to read and was handed a scroll of the
    prophet Isaiah.

He unrolled the scroll and found the passage where it
   was written:
   The Spirit of the Lord is upon me,
      because he has anointed me
      to bring glad tidings to the poor.
   He has sent me to proclaim liberty to captives
      and recovery of sight to the blind,
      to let the oppressed go free,
      and to proclaim a year acceptable to the Lord.
Rolling up the scroll, he handed it back to the attendant
   and sat down,
   and the eyes of all in the synagogue looked intently
      at him.
He said to them,
   "Today this Scripture passage is fulfilled in
      your hearing."

The Gospel of the Lord.

Fourth Sunday in Ordinary Time

Like Elijah and Elisha, Jesus was not sent only to the Jews.

A reading from the holy Gospel according to Luke

4:21–30

Jesus began speaking in the synagogue, saying:
  "Today this Scripture passage is fulfilled in
    your hearing."
And all spoke highly of him
  and were amazed at the gracious words that came
    from his mouth.
They also asked, "Isn't this the son of Joseph?"
He said to them, "Surely you will quote me this proverb,
  'Physician, cure yourself,' and say,
  'Do here in your native place
  the things that we heard were done in Capernaum.'"
And he said, "Amen, I say to you,
  no prophet is accepted in his own native place.
Indeed, I tell you,
  there were many widows in Israel in the days of Elijah
  when the sky was closed for three and a half years
  and a severe famine spread over the entire land.
It was to none of these that Elijah was sent,
  but only to a widow in Zarephath in the land of Sidon.
Again, there were many lepers in Israel
  during the time of Elisha the prophet;

yet not one of them was cleansed, but only Naaman
    the Syrian."
When the people in the synagogue heard this,
    they were all filled with fury.
They rose up, drove him out of the town,
    and led him to the brow of the hill
    on which their town had been built,
    to hurl him down headlong.
But Jesus passed through the midst of them and
    went away.

The Gospel of the Lord.

February 4, 2007

FIFTH SUNDAY IN ORDINARY TIME

They left everything and followed Jesus.

A reading from the holy Gospel according to Luke

5:1–11

While the crowd was pressing in on Jesus and listening
    to the word of God,
    he was standing by the Lake of Gennesaret.
He saw two boats there alongside the lake;
    the fishermen had disembarked and were washing
    their nets.

Getting into one of the boats, the one belonging
to Simon,
he asked him to put out a short distance from the shore.
Then he sat down and taught the crowds from the boat.
After he had finished speaking, he said to Simon,
"Put out into deep water and lower your nets for
a catch."
Simon said in reply,
"Master, we have worked hard all night and have
caught nothing,
but at your command I will lower the nets."
When they had done this, they caught a great number
of fish
and their nets were tearing.
They signaled to their partners in the other boat
to come to help them.
They came and filled both boats
so that the boats were in danger of sinking.
When Simon Peter saw this, he fell at the knees of Jesus
and said,
"Depart from me, Lord, for I am a sinful man."
For astonishment at the catch of fish they had made
seized him
and all those with him,
and likewise James and John, the sons of Zebedee,
who were partners of Simon.
Jesus said to Simon, "Do not be afraid;
from now on you will be catching men."

When they brought their boats to the shore,
   they left everything and followed him.

The Gospel of the Lord.

February 11, 2007

Sixth Sunday in Ordinary Time

Blessed are the poor. Woe to you who are rich.

A reading from the holy Gospel according to Luke   6:17, 20–26

Jesus came down with the twelve
   and stood on a stretch of level ground
   with a great crowd of his disciples
   and a large number of the people
   from all Judea and Jerusalem
   and the coastal region of Tyre and Sidon.
And raising his eyes toward his disciples he said:
   "Blessed are you who are poor,
      for the kingdom of God is yours.
   Blessed are you who are now hungry,
      for you will be satisfied.
   Blessed are you who are now weeping,
      for you will laugh.
   Blessed are you when people hate you,
      and when they exclude and insult you,

and denounce your name as evil
on account of the Son of Man.
Rejoice and leap for joy on that day!
Behold, your reward will be great in heaven.
For their ancestors treated the prophets in the same way.
But woe to you who are rich,
for you have received your consolation.
Woe to you who are filled now,
for you will be hungry.
Woe to you who laugh now,
for you will grieve and weep.
Woe to you when all speak well of you,
for their ancestors treated the false prophets in
this way."

The Gospel of the Lord.

February 18, 2007

SEVENTH SUNDAY IN ORDINARY TIME

Be merciful, just as your father is merciful.

A reading from the holy Gospel according to Luke

6:27–38

Jesus said to his disciples:
"To you who hear I say,
love your enemies, do good to those who hate you,

bless those who curse you, pray for those who
   mistreat you.
To the person who strikes you on one cheek,
   offer the other one as well,
   and from the person who takes your cloak,
   do not withhold even your tunic.
Give to everyone who asks of you,
   and from the one who takes what is yours do not
      demand it back.
Do to others as you would have them do to you.
For if you love those who love you,
   what credit is that to you?
Even sinners love those who love them.
And if you do good to those who do good to you,
   what credit is that to you?
Even sinners do the same.
If you lend money to those from whom you expect
      repayment,
   what credit is that to you?
Even sinners lend to sinners,
   and get back the same amount.
But rather, love your enemies and do good to them,
   and lend expecting nothing back;
   then your reward will be great
   and you will be children of the Most High,
   for he himself is kind to the ungrateful and the wicked.
Be merciful, just as your Father is merciful.

"Stop judging and you will not be judged.
Stop condemning and you will not be condemned.
Forgive and you will be forgiven.
Give and gifts will be given to you;
    a good measure, packed together, shaken down,
        and overflowing,
    will be poured into your lap.
For the measure with which you measure
    will in return be measured out to you."

The Gospel of the Lord.

February 25, 2007

FIRST SUNDAY OF LENT

Jesus was led by the Spirit into the desert and was tempted.

A reading from the holy Gospel according to Luke

4:1–13

Filled with the Holy Spirit, Jesus returned from
    the Jordan
  and was led by the Spirit into the desert for forty days,
    to be tempted by the devil.
He ate nothing during those days,
    and when they were over he was hungry.
The devil said to him,
"If you are the Son of God,
    command this stone to become bread."

Jesus answered him,
"It is written, *One does not live on bread alone.*"
Then he took him up and showed him
  all the kingdoms of the world in a single instant.
The devil said to him,
"I shall give to you all this power and glory;
  for it has been handed over to me,
  and I may give it to whomever I wish.
All this will be yours, if you worship me."
Jesus said to him in reply,
"It is written:
  You shall worship the Lord, your God,
    and him alone shall you serve."
Then he led him to Jerusalem,
  made him stand on the parapet of the temple, and said
    to him,
"If you are the Son of God,
  throw yourself down from here, for it is written:
    He will command his angels concerning you,
      to guard you,
  and:
    With their hands they will support you,
    lest you dash your foot against a stone."
Jesus said to him in reply,
  "It also says,
  You shall not put the Lord, your God, to the test."

When the devil had finished every temptation,
  he departed from him for a time.

The Gospel of the Lord.

March 4, 2007

SECOND SUNDAY OF LENT

*While he was praying, his face changed in appearance and his clothing
became dazzling white.*

A reading from the holy Gospel according to Luke
                                                           9:28b–36

Jesus took Peter, John and James
  and went up the mountain to pray.
While he was praying, his face changed in appearance
  and his clothing became dazzling white.
And behold, two men were conversing with him, Moses
      and Elijah,
    who appeared in glory and spoke of his exodus
    that he was going to accomplish in Jerusalem.
Peter and his companions had been overcome by sleep,
  but becoming fully awake,
    they saw his glory and the two men standing with him.
As they were about to part from him, Peter said to Jesus,
    "Master, it is good that we are here;
    let us make three tents,
    one for you, one for Moses, and one for Elijah."

But he did not know what he was saying.
While he was still speaking,
   a cloud came and cast a shadow over them,
   and they became frightened when they entered
      the cloud.
Then from the cloud came a voice that said,
   "This is my chosen Son; listen to him."
After the voice had spoken, Jesus was found alone.
They fell silent and did not at that time
   tell anyone what they had seen.

The Gospel of the Lord.

March 11, 2007

THIRD SUNDAY OF LENT

If you do not repent, you will all perish as they did.

A reading from the holy Gospel according to Luke

13:1–9

Some people told Jesus about the Galileans
   whose blood Pilate had mingled with the blood
      of their sacrifices.

Jesus said to them in reply,
   "Do you think that because these Galileans suffered
      in this way
   they were greater sinners than all other Galileans?

By no means!
But I tell you, if you do not repent,
   you will all perish as they did!
Or those eighteen people who were killed
   when the tower at Siloam fell on them—
   do you think they were more guilty
   than everyone else who lived in Jerusalem?
By no means!
But I tell you, if you do not repent,
   you will all perish as they did!"

And he told them this parable:
   "There once was a person who had a fig tree planted
      in his orchard,
   and when he came in search of fruit on it but
      found none,
   he said to the gardener,
   'For three years now I have come in search of fruit
      on this fig tree
   but have found none.
So cut it down.
Why should it exhaust the soil?'
He said to him in reply,
   'Sir, leave it for this year also,
   and I shall cultivate the ground around it and fertilize it;
   it may bear fruit in the future.
If not you can cut it down.'"

The Gospel of the Lord.

March 18, 2007

FOURTH SUNDAY OF LENT

Your brother was dead and has come to life again.

A reading from the holy Gospel according to Luke
15:1–3, 11–32

Tax collectors and sinners were all drawing near to listen
    to Jesus,
  but the Pharisees and scribes began to complain,
    saying,
  "This man welcomes sinners and eats with them."
So to them Jesus addressed this parable:
"A man had two sons, and the younger son said to
    his father,
  'Father give me the share of your estate that should
    come to me.'
So the father divided the property between them.
After a few days, the younger son collected all
    his belongings
  and set off to a distant country
  where he squandered his inheritance on a life
    of dissipation.
When he had freely spent everything,
  a severe famine struck that country,
  and he found himself in dire need.
So he hired himself out to one of the local citizens
  who sent him to his farm to tend the swine.

And he longed to eat his fill of the pods on which the
     swine fed,
   but nobody gave him any.
Coming to his senses he thought,
   'How many of my father's hired workers
   have more than enough food to eat,
   but here am I, dying from hunger.
I shall get up and go to my father and I shall say to him,
   "Father, I have sinned against heaven and against you.
I no longer deserve to be called your son;
   treat me as you would treat one of your
      hired workers."'
So he got up and went back to his father.
While he was still a long way off,
   his father caught sight of him, and was filled
      with compassion.
He ran to his son, embraced him and kissed him.
His son said to him,
   'Father, I have sinned against heaven and against you;
   I no longer deserve to be called your son.'
But his father ordered his servants,
   'Quickly bring the finest robe and put it on him;
   put a ring on his finger and sandals on his feet.
Take the fattened calf and slaughter it.
Then let us celebrate with a feast,
   because this son of mine was dead, and has come to
      life again;
   he was lost, and has been found.'
Then the celebration began.

Now the older son had been out in the field
    and, on his way back, as he neared the house,
    he heard the sound of music and dancing.
He called one of the servants and asked what this
        might mean.
The servant said to him,
    'Your brother has returned
    and your father has slaughtered the fattened calf
    because he has him back safe and sound.'
He became angry,
    and when he refused to enter the house,
    his father came out and pleaded with him.
He said to his father in reply,
    'Look, all these years I served you
    and not once did I disobey your orders;
    yet you never gave me even a young goat
        to feast on with my friends.
But when your son returns
    who swallowed up your property with prostitutes,
    for him you slaughter the fattened calf.'
He said to him,
    'My son, you are here with me always;
    everything I have is yours.
But now we must celebrate and rejoice,
    because your brother was dead and has come to
        life again;
    he was lost and has been found.'"

The Gospel of the Lord.

March 25, 2007

Fifth Sunday of Lent

*Let the one among you who is without sin be the first to throw a stone
at her.*

A reading from the holy Gospel according to John

8:1–11

Jesus went to the Mount of Olives.
But early in the morning he arrived again in the
temple area,
and all the people started coming to him,
and he sat down and taught them.
Then the scribes and the Pharisees brought a woman
who had been caught in adultery
and made her stand in the middle.
They said to him,
"Teacher, this woman was caught
in the very act of committing adultery.
Now in the law, Moses commanded us to stone
such women.
So what do you say?"
They said this to test him,
so that they could have some charge to bring
against him.
Jesus bent down and began to write on the ground with
his finger.
But when they continued asking him,
he straightened up and said to them,

"Let the one among you who is without sin
be the first to throw a stone at her."
Again he bent down and wrote on the ground.
And in response, they went away one by one,
beginning with the elders.
So he was left alone with the woman before him.
Then Jesus straightened up and said to her,
"Woman, where are they?
Has no one condemned you?"
She replied, "No one, sir."
Then Jesus said, "Neither do I condemn you.
Go, and from now on do not sin any more."

The Gospel of the Lord.

April 1, 2007

PALM SUNDAY OF
THE LORD'S PASSION

The Passion of our Lord Jesus Christ.
The Passion of our Lord Jesus Christ
    according to Luke   *23:1–49*
Then the whole assembly of them arose and brought him
    before Pilate.
They brought charges against him, saying,
    "We found this man misleading our people;
    he opposes the payment of taxes to Caesar
    and maintains that he is the Christ, a king."

Pilate asked him, "Are you the king of the Jews?"
He said to him in reply, "You say so."
Pilate then addressed the chief priests and the crowds,
    "I find this man not guilty."
But they were adamant and said,
    "He is inciting the people with his teaching
        throughout all Judea,
    from Galilee where he began even to here."
On hearing this Pilate asked if the man was a Galilean;
    and upon learning that he was under
        Herod's jurisdiction,
    he sent him to Herod, who was in Jerusalem at
        that time.
Herod was very glad to see Jesus;
    he had been wanting to see him for a long time,
    for he had heard about him
    and had been hoping to see him perform some sign.
He questioned him at length,
    but he gave him no answer.
The chief priests and scribes, meanwhile,
    stood by accusing him harshly.
Herod and his soldiers treated him contemptuously
        and mocked him,
    and after clothing him in resplendent garb,
    he sent him back to Pilate.
Herod and Pilate became friends that very day,
    even though they had been enemies formerly.
Pilate then summoned the chief priests, the rulers
        and the people

and said to them, "You brought this man to me
    and accused him of inciting the people to revolt.
I have conducted my investigation in your presence
    and have not found this man guilty
    of the charges you have brought against him,
    nor did Herod, for he sent him back to us.
So no capital crime has been committed by him.
Therefore I shall have him flogged and then release him."

But all together they shouted out,
    "Away with this man!
    Release Barabbas to us."
— Now Barabbas had been imprisoned for a rebellion
    that had taken place in the city and for murder. —
Again Pilate addressed them, still wishing to
        release Jesus,
    but they continued their shouting,
    "Crucify him! Crucify him!"
Pilate addressed them a third time,
    "What evil has this man done?
    I found him guilty of no capital crime.
Therefore I shall have him flogged and then release him."
With loud shouts, however,
    they persisted in calling for his crucifixion,
    and their voices prevailed.
The verdict of Pilate was that their demand
        should be granted.
So he released the man who had been imprisoned
    for rebellion and murder, for whom they asked,

and he handed Jesus over to them to deal with
    as they wished.

As they led him away
    they took hold of a certain Simon, a Cyrenian,
    who was coming in from the country;
    and after laying the cross on him,
    they made him carry it behind Jesus.
A large crowd of people followed Jesus,
    including many women who mourned
        and lamented him.
Jesus turned to them and said,
    "Daughters of Jerusalem, do not weep for me;
    weep instead for yourselves and for your children
    for indeed, the days are coming when people will say,
    'Blessed are the barren,
    the wombs that never bore
    and the breasts that never nursed.'
At that time people will say to the mountains,
    'Fall upon us!'
    and to the hills, 'Cover us!'
    for if these things are done when the wood is green,
    what will happen when it is dry?"
Now two others, both criminals,
    were led away with him to be executed.

When they came to the place called the Skull,
    they crucified him and the criminals there,
    one on his right, the other on his left.

Then Jesus said,
   "Father, forgive them, they know not what they do."
They divided his garments by casting lots.
The people stood by and watched;
   the rulers, meanwhile, sneered at him and said,
   "He saved others, let him save himself
   if he is the chosen one, the Christ of God."
Even the soldiers jeered at him.
As they approached to offer him wine they called out,
   "If you are King of the Jews, save yourself."
Above him there was an inscription that read,
   "This is the King of the Jews."

Now one of the criminals hanging there reviled Jesus,
      saying,
   "Are you not the Christ?
   Save yourself and us."
The other, however, rebuking him, said in reply,
   "Have you no fear of God,
   for you are subject to the same condemnation?
And indeed, we have been condemned justly,
   for the sentence we received corresponds to
      our crimes,
   but this man has done nothing criminal."
Then he said,
   "Jesus, remember me when you come into
      your kingdom."
He replied to him,
   "Amen, I say to you,
   today you will be with me in Paradise."

It was now about noon and darkness came over
    the whole land
  until three in the afternoon
  because of an eclipse of the sun.
Then the veil of the temple was torn down the middle.
Jesus cried out in a loud voice,
  "Father, into your hands I commend my spirit";
  and when he had said this he breathed his last.

Here all kneel and pause for a short time.

The centurion who witnessed what had happened
    glorified God and said,
  "This man was innocent beyond doubt."
When all the people who had gathered for this spectacle
    saw what had happened,
  they returned home beating their breasts;
  but all his acquaintances stood at a distance,
  including the women who had followed him
    from Galilee
  and saw these events.

The Gospel of the Lord.

Shorter form

April 8, 2007

Easter Sunday: The Resurrection of the Lord

He had to rise from the dead.

A reading from the holy Gospel according to John

20:1–9

On the first day of the week,
   Mary of Magdala came to the tomb early in
      the morning,
   while it was still dark,
   and saw the stone removed from the tomb.
So she ran and went to Simon Peter
   and to the other disciple whom Jesus loved, and
      told them,
   "They have taken the Lord from the tomb,
   and we don't know where they put him."
So Peter and the other disciple went out and came to
      the tomb.
They both ran, but the other disciple ran faster than Peter
   and arrived at the tomb first;
   he bent down and saw the burial cloths there, but did
      not go in.
When Simon Peter arrived after him,
   he went into the tomb and saw the burial cloths there,
   and the cloth that had covered his head,
   not with the burial cloths but rolled up in
      a separate place.

Then the other disciple also went in,
    the one who had arrived at the tomb first,
    and he saw and believed.
For they did not yet understand the Scripture
    that he had to rise from the dead.

The Gospel of the Lord.

April 15, 2007

SECOND SUNDAY OF EASTER/ DIVINE MERCY SUNDAY

Eight days later Jesus came and stood in their midst.

A reading from the holy Gospel according to John

20:19–31

On the evening of that first day of the week,
    when the doors were locked, where the disciples were,
    for fear of the Jews,
    Jesus came and stood in their midst
    and said to them, "Peace be with you."
When he had said this, he showed them his hands and
    his side.
The disciples rejoiced when they saw the Lord.
Jesus said to them again, "Peace be with you.
As the Father has sent me, so I send you."

And when he had said this, he breathed on them and
    said to them,
  "Receive the Holy Spirit.
Whose sins you forgive are forgiven them,
  and whose sins you retain are retained."

Thomas, called Didymus, one of the Twelve,
  was not with them when Jesus came.
So the other disciples said to him, "We have seen
    the Lord."
But he said to them,
  "Unless I see the mark of the nails in his hands
  and put my finger into the nailmarks
  and put my hand into his side, I will not believe."

Now a week later his disciples were again inside
  and Thomas was with them.
Jesus came, although the doors were locked,
  and stood in their midst and said, "Peace be with you."
Then he said to Thomas, "Put your finger here and see
    my hands,
  and bring your hand and put it into my side,
  and do not be unbelieving, but believe."
Thomas answered and said to him, "My Lord and
    my God!"
Jesus said to him, "Have you come to believe
    because you have seen me?
Blessed are those who have not seen and have believed."

Now Jesus did many other signs in the presence of
    his disciples
  that are not written in this book.
But these are written that you may come to believe
    that Jesus is the Christ, the Son of God,
    and that through this belief you may have life in
      his name.

The Gospel of the Lord.

April 22, 2007

Third Sunday of Easter

*Jesus came and took the bread and gave it to them, and in like manner,
the fish.*

A reading from the holy Gospel according to John

21:1–14

At that time, Jesus revealed himself again
    to his disciples at the Sea of Tiberias.
He revealed himself in this way.
Together were Simon Peter, Thomas called Didymus,
    Nathanael from Cana in Galilee,
    Zebedee's sons, and two others of his disciples.
Simon Peter said to them, "I am going fishing."
They said to him, "We also will come with you."
So they went out and got into the boat,
    but that night they caught nothing.

When it was already dawn, Jesus was standing
    on the shore;
  but the disciples did not realize that it was Jesus.
Jesus said to them, "Children, have you caught
    anything to eat?"
They answered him, "No."
So he said to them, "Cast the net over the right side
    of the boat
  and you will find something."
So they cast it, and were not able to pull it in
    because of the number of fish.

So the disciple whom Jesus loved said to Peter,
    "It is the Lord."
When Simon Peter heard that it was the Lord,
  he tucked in his garment, for he was lightly clad,
  and jumped into the sea.
The other disciples came in the boat,
  for they were not far from shore, only about
    a hundred yards,
  dragging the net with the fish.
When they climbed out on shore,
  they saw a charcoal fire with fish on it and bread.
Jesus said to them, "Bring some of the fish
    you just caught."
So Simon Peter went over and dragged the net ashore
  full of one hundred fifty-three large fish.
Even though there were so many, the net was not torn.
Jesus said to them, "Come, have breakfast."

And none of the disciples dared to ask him,
  "Who are you?"
  because they realized it was the Lord.
Jesus came over and took the bread and gave it to them,
  and in like manner the fish.
This was now the third time Jesus was revealed
    to his disciples
  after being raised from the dead.

The Gospel of the Lord.

April 29, 2007

FOURTH SUNDAY OF EASTER

I give my sheep eternal life.

A reading from the holy Gospel according to John
10:27–30

Jesus said:
"My sheep hear my voice;
  I know them, and they follow me.
I give them eternal life, and they shall never perish.
No one can take them out of my hand.
My Father, who has given them to me, is greater than all,
  and no one can take them out of the Father's hand.
The Father and I are one."

The Gospel of the Lord.

May 6, 2007

Fifth Sunday of Easter

I give you a new commandment: Love one another.

A reading from the holy Gospel according to John

13:31–33a, 34–35

When Judas had left them, Jesus said,
  "Now is the Son of Man glorified, and God is
    glorified in him.
If God is glorified in him,
  God will also glorify him in himself,
  and God will glorify him at once.
My children, I will be with you only a little
    while longer.
I give you a new commandment: love one another.
As I have loved you, so you also should love
    one another.
This is how all will know that you are my disciples,
  if you have love for one another."

The Gospel of the Lord.

May 13, 2007

Sixth Sunday of Easter

The Holy Spirit will teach you everything and remind you of all that I told you.

A reading from the holy Gospel according to John

14:23–29

Jesus said to his disciples:
   "Whoever loves me will keep my word,
   and my Father will love him,
   and we will come to him and make our dwelling
     with him.
Whoever does not love me does not keep my words;
   yet the word you hear is not mine
   but that of the Father who sent me.

"I have told you this while I am with you.
The Advocate, the Holy Spirit,
   whom the Father will send in my name,
   will teach you everything
   and remind you of all that I told you.
Peace I leave with you; my peace I give to you.
Not as the world gives do I give it to you.
Do not let your hearts be troubled or afraid.
You heard me tell you,
   'I am going away and I will come back to you.'
If you loved me,
   you would rejoice that I am going to the Father;
   for the Father is greater than I.

And now I have told you this before it happens,
   so that when it happens you may believe."

The Gospel of the Lord.

May 17, 2007

ASCENSION OF THE LORD

As he blessed them, he was taken up to heaven.

A reading from the holy Gospel according to Luke

24:46–53

Jesus said to his disciples:
"Thus it is written that the Christ would suffer
   and rise from the dead on the third day
   and that repentance, for the forgiveness of sins,
   would be preached in his name
   to all the nations, beginning from Jerusalem.
You are witnesses of these things.
And behold I am sending the promise of my Father
      upon you;
   but stay in the city
   until you are clothed with power from on high."

Then he led them out as far as Bethany,
   raised his hands, and blessed them.
As he blessed them he parted from them
   and was taken up to heaven.

They did him homage
   and then returned to Jerusalem with great joy,
   and they were continually in the temple praising God.

The Gospel of the Lord.

May 20, 2007

SEVENTH SUNDAY OF EASTER

That they may be brought to perfection as one!

A reading from the holy Gospel according to John

17:20–26

Lifting up his eyes to heaven, Jesus prayed saying:
"Holy Father, I pray not only for them,
   but also for those who will believe in me through
      their word,
   so that they may all be one,
   as you, Father, are in me and I in you,
   that they also may be in us,
   that the world may believe that you sent me.
And I have given them the glory you gave me,
   so that they may be one, as we are one,
   I in them and you in me,
   that they may be brought to perfection as one,
   that the world may know that you sent me,
   and that you loved them even as you loved me.
Father, they are your gift to me.

I wish that where I am they also may be with me,
  that they may see my glory that you gave me,
  because you loved me before the foundation of
    the world.
Righteous Father, the world also does not know you,
  but I know you, and they know that you sent me.
I made known to them your name and I will make
    it known,
  that the love with which you loved me
  may be in them and I in them."

The Gospel of the Lord.

In the dioceses where today is celebrated as the Ascension of the Lord, refer to the readings for May 17, 2007 on page 83.

May 27, 2007

PENTECOST SUNDAY

The Holy Spirit will teach you everything.

A reading from the holy Gospel according to John
14:15–16, 23b–26

Jesus said to his disciples:
"If you love me, you will keep my commandments.
And I will ask the Father,
  and he will give you another Advocate to be with
    you always.

"Whoever loves me will keep my word,
   and my Father will love him,
   and we will come to him and make our dwelling
      with him.
Those who do not love me do not keep my words;
   yet the word you hear is not mine
   but that of the Father who sent me.

"I have told you this while I am with you.
The Advocate, the Holy Spirit whom the Father
      will send in my name,
   will teach you everything
   and remind you of all that I told you."

The Gospel of the Lord.

The Gospel from Year A (John 20:19–23) may also be used.

June 3, 2007

THE MOST HOLY TRINITY

Everything that the Father has is mine; the Spirit will take from what is mine and declare it to you.

A reading from the holy Gospel according to John   *16:12–15*

Jesus said to his disciples:
"I have much more to tell you, but you cannot bear
      it now.

But when he comes, the Spirit of truth,
    he will guide you to all truth.
He will not speak on his own,
    but he will speak what he hears,
    and will declare to you the things that are coming.
He will glorify me,
    because he will take from what is mine and declare
        it to you.
Everything that the Father has is mine;
    for this reason I told you that he will take from what
        is mine
    and declare it to you."

The Gospel of the Lord.

June 10, 2007

THE MOST HOLY BODY AND BLOOD OF CHRIST

They all ate and were satisfied.

A reading from the holy Gospel according to Luke

9:11b–17

Jesus spoke to the crowds about the kingdom of God,
    and he healed those who needed to be cured.
As the day was drawing to a close,
    the Twelve approached him and said,
    "Dismiss the crowd

so that they can go to the surrounding villages
and farms
and find lodging and provisions;
for we are in a deserted place here."
He said to them, "Give them some food yourselves."
They replied, "Five loaves and two fish are all we have,
unless we ourselves go and buy food for all
these people."
Now the men there numbered about five thousand.
Then he said to his disciples,
"Have them sit down in groups of about fifty."
They did so and made them all sit down.
Then taking the five loaves and the two fish,
and looking up to heaven,
he said the blessing over them, broke them,
and gave them to the disciples to set before the crowd.
They all ate and were satisfied.
And when the leftover fragments were picked up,
they filled twelve wicker baskets.

The Gospel of the Lord.

June 17, 2007

Eleventh Sunday in Ordinary Time

Her many sins have been forgiven, because she has shown great love.

A reading from the holy Gospel according to Luke
7:36–50

A Pharisee invited Jesus to dine with him,
   and he entered the Pharisee's house
      and reclined at table.

Now there was a sinful woman in the city
   who learned that he was at table in the house
      of the Pharisee.
Bringing an alabaster flask of ointment,
   she stood behind him at his feet weeping
   and began to bathe his feet with her tears.
Then she wiped them with her hair,
   kissed them, and anointed them with the ointment.
When the Pharisee who had invited him saw this
      he said to himself,
   "If this man were a prophet,
   he would know who and what sort of woman this is
      who is touching him,
   that she is a sinner."
Jesus said to him in reply,
   "Simon, I have something to say to you."
"Tell me, teacher," he said.

"Two people were in debt to a certain creditor;
    one owed five hundred days' wages and the other
        owed fifty.
Since they were unable to repay the debt,
    he forgave it for both.
Which of them will love him more?"
Simon said in reply,
    "The one, I suppose, whose larger debt was forgiven."
He said to him, "You have judged rightly."

Then he turned to the woman and said to Simon,
    "Do you see this woman?
When I entered your house, you did not give me water
        for my feet,
    but she has bathed them with her tears
    and wiped them with her hair.
You did not give me a kiss,
    but she has not ceased kissing my feet since the time
        I entered.
You did not anoint my head with oil,
    but she anointed my feet with ointment.
So I tell you, her many sins have been forgiven
    because she has shown great love.
But the one to whom little is forgiven, loves little."
He said to her, "Your sins are forgiven."
The others at table said to themselves,
    "Who is this who even forgives sins?"

But he said to the woman,
  "Your faith has saved you; go in peace."

The Gospel of the Lord.

Shorter form

June 24, 2007

THE NATIVITY OF SAINT JOHN THE BAPTIST

John is his name.

A reading from the holy Gospel according to Luke   *1:57–66, 80*

When the time arrived for Elizabeth to have her child
  she gave birth to a son.
Her neighbors and relatives heard
  that the Lord had shown his great mercy toward her,
  and they rejoiced with her.
When they came on the eighth day to circumcise
    the child,
  they were going to call him Zechariah after his father,
  but his mother said in reply,
  "No. He will be called John."
But they answered her,
  "There is no one among your relatives
    who has this name."

So they made signs, asking his father what he wished him
     to be called.
He asked for a tablet and wrote, "John is his name,"
   and all were amazed.
Immediately his mouth was opened, his tongue freed,
   and he spoke blessing God.
Then fear came upon all their neighbors,
   and all these matters were discussed
   throughout the hill country of Judea.
All who heard these things took them to heart, saying,
   "What, then, will this child be?"
For surely the hand of the Lord was with him.
The child grew and became strong in spirit,
   and he was in the desert until the day
   of his manifestation to Israel.

The Gospel of the Lord.

July 1, 2007

THIRTEENTH SUNDAY
IN ORDINARY TIME

*He resolutely determined to journey to Jerusalem. I will follow you
wherever you go.*

A reading from the holy Gospel
according to Luke

9:51–62

When the days for Jesus' being taken up were fulfilled,

he resolutely determined to journey to Jerusalem,
and he sent messengers ahead of him.
On the way they entered a Samaritan village
to prepare for his reception there,
but they would not welcome him
because the destination of his journey was Jerusalem.
When the disciples James and John saw this they asked,
"Lord, do you want us to call down fire from heaven
to consume them?"
Jesus turned and rebuked them, and they journeyed
to another village.
As they were proceeding on their journey someone said
to him,
"I will follow you wherever you go."
Jesus answered him,
"Foxes have dens and birds of the sky have nests,
but the Son of Man has nowhere to rest his head."

And to another he said, "Follow me."
But he replied, "Lord, let me go first and bury my father."
But he answered him, "Let the dead bury their dead.
But you, go and proclaim the kingdom of God."
And another said, "I will follow you, Lord,
but first let me say farewell to my family at home."
To him Jesus said, "No one who sets a hand to the plow
and looks to what was left behind is fit for the
kingdom of God."

The Gospel of the Lord.

July 8, 2007

Fourteenth Sunday in Ordinary Time

Your peace will rest on that person.

A reading from the holy Gospel according to Luke

10:1–9

At that time the Lord appointed seventy-two others
   whom he sent ahead of him in pairs
   to every town and place he intended to visit.
He said to them,
   "The harvest is abundant but the laborers are few;
   so ask the master of the harvest
   to send out laborers for his harvest.
Go on your way;
   behold, I am sending you like lambs among wolves.
Carry no money bag, no sack, no sandals;
   and greet no one along the way.
Into whatever house you enter, first say,
   'Peace to this household.'
If a peaceful person lives there,
   your peace will rest on him;
   but if not, it will return to you.
Stay in the same house and eat and drink what is
      offered to you,
   for the laborer deserves his payment.
Do not move about from one house to another.

Whatever town you enter and they welcome you,
  eat what is set before you,
  cure the sick in it and say to them,
  'The kingdom of God is at hand for you.'

The Gospel of the Lord.

Shorter form

July 15, 2007

FIFTEENTH SUNDAY IN ORDINARY TIME

Who is my neighbor?

A reading from the holy Gospel according to Luke

10:25–37

There was a scholar of the law who stood up to test him
    and said,
  "Teacher, what must I do to inherit eternal life?"
Jesus said to him, "What is written in the law?
How do you read it?"
He said in reply,
  "You shall love the Lord, your God,
  with all your heart,
  with all your being,
  with all your strength,

and with all your mind,
and your neighbor as yourself."

He replied to him, "You have answered correctly;
  do this and you will live."

But because he wished to justify himself, he said
    to Jesus,
  "And who is my neighbor?"
Jesus replied,
  "A man fell victim to robbers
  as he went down from Jerusalem to Jericho.
They stripped and beat him and went off leaving
    him half-dead.
A priest happened to be going down that road,
  but when he saw him, he passed by on the
    opposite side.
Likewise a Levite came to the place,
  and when he saw him, he passed by on the
    opposite side.
But a Samaritan traveler who came upon him
  was moved with compassion at the sight.
He approached the victim,
  poured oil and wine over his wounds and
    bandaged them.
Then he lifted him up on his own animal,
  took him to an inn, and cared for him.
"The next day he took out two silver coins
  and gave them to the innkeeper with the instruction,
  'Take care of him.

If you spend more than what I have given you,
   I shall repay you on my way back.'
Which of these three, in your opinion,
   was neighbor to the robbers' victim?"
He answered, "The one who treated him with mercy."
Jesus said to him, "Go and do likewise."

The Gospel of the Lord.

July 22, 2007

SIXTEENTH SUNDAY IN ORDINARY TIME

Martha welcomed him. Mary has chosen the better part.

A reading from the holy Gospel according to Luke   *10:38 – 42*

Jesus entered a village
   where a woman whose name was Martha
      welcomed him.
She had a sister named Mary
   who sat beside the Lord at his feet listening to
      him speak.
Martha, burdened with much serving, came to him
      and said,
   "Lord, do you not care
   that my sister has left me by myself to do the serving?
Tell her to help me."

The Lord said to her in reply,
  "Martha, Martha, you are anxious and worried
    about many things.
There is need of only one thing.
Mary has chosen the better part
  and it will not be taken from her."

The Gospel of the Lord.

July 29, 2007

Seventeenth Sunday in Ordinary Time

Ask and you will receive.

A reading from the holy Gospel according to Luke

11:1–13

Jesus was praying in a certain place, and when he
    had finished,
  one of his disciples said to him,
  "Lord, teach us to pray just as John taught
    his disciples."
He said to them, "When you pray, say:
  Father, hallowed be your name,
    your kingdom come.
    Give us each day our daily bread
    and forgive us our sins

for we ourselves forgive everyone in debt to us,
    and do not subject us to the final test.''

And he said to them, "Suppose one of you has a friend
    to whom he goes at midnight and says,
    'Friend, lend me three loaves of bread,
    for a friend of mine has arrived at my house from
      a journey
    and I have nothing to offer him,'
    and he says in reply from within,
    'Do not bother me; the door has already been locked
    and my children and I are already in bed.
I cannot get up to give you anything.'
I tell you,
    if he does not get up to give the visitor the loaves
    because of their friendship,
    he will get up to give him whatever he needs
    because of his persistence.

"And I tell you, ask and you will receive;
    seek and you will find;
    knock and the door will be opened to you.
For everyone who asks, receives;
    and the one who seeks, finds;
    and to the one who knocks, the door will be opened.
What father among you would hand his son a snake
    when he asks for a fish?
Or hand him a scorpion when he asks for an egg?
If you then, who are wicked,
    know how to give good gifts to your children,

how much more will the Father in heaven
give the Holy Spirit to those who ask him?"

The Gospel of the Lord.

August 5, 2007

EIGHTEENTH SUNDAY
IN ORDINARY TIME

The things you have prepared, to whom will they belong?

A reading from the holy Gospel
according to Luke

12:13–21

Someone in the crowd said to Jesus,
    "Teacher, tell my brother to share the inheritance
        with me."
He replied to him,
    "Friend, who appointed me as your judge
        and arbitrator?"
Then he said to the crowd,
    "Take care to guard against all greed,
    for though one may be rich,
    one's life does not consist of possessions."

Then he told them a parable.
"There was a rich man whose land produced
        a bountiful harvest.

He asked himself, 'What shall I do,
   for I do not have space to store my harvest?'
And he said, 'This is what I shall do:
   I shall tear down my barns and build larger ones.
There I shall store all my grain and other goods
   and I shall say to myself, "Now as for you,
   you have so many good things stored up for
      many years,
   rest, eat, drink, be merry!"'
But God said to him,
   'You fool, this night your life will be demanded
      of you;
   and the things you have prepared, to whom will
      they belong?'
Thus will it be for all who store up treasure
      for themselves
   but are not rich in what matters to God."

The Gospel of the Lord.

August 12, 2007

Nineteenth Sunday in Ordinary Time

You also must be prepared.

A reading from the holy Gospel according to Luke 12:35-40

Jesus said to his disciples:
"Gird your loins and light your lamps
   and be like servants who await their master's return
      from a wedding,
   ready to open immediately when he comes
      and knocks.
Blessed are those servants
   whom the master finds vigilant on his arrival.
Amen, I say to you, he will gird himself,
   have them recline at table, and proceed to wait
      on them.
And should he come in the second or third watch
   and find them prepared in this way,
   blessed are those servants.
Be sure of this:
   if the master of the house had known the hour
   when the thief was coming,
   he would not have let his house be broken into.

You also must be prepared, for at an hour
    you do not expect,
  the Son of Man will come."

The Gospel of the Lord.

Shorter form

August 15, 2007

THE ASSUMPTION OF THE BLESSED VIRGIN MARY

The Almighty has done great things for me; he has raised up the lowly.

A reading from the holy Gospel according to Luke

1:39–56

Mary set out
  and traveled to the hill country in haste
  to a town of Judah,
  where she entered the house of Zechariah
  and greeted Elizabeth.
When Elizabeth heard Mary's greeting,
  the infant leaped in her womb,
  and Elizabeth, filled with the Holy Spirit,
  cried out in a loud voice and said,
  "Blessed are you among women,
  and blessed is the fruit of your womb.

And how does this happen to me,
  that the mother of my Lord should come to me?
For at the moment the sound of your greeting reached
    my ears,
  the infant in my womb leaped for joy.
Blessed are you who believed
  that what was spoken to you by the Lord
  would be fulfilled."

And Mary said:
  "My soul proclaims the greatness of the Lord;
    my spirit rejoices in God my Savior
    for he has looked upon his lowly servant.
  From this day all generations will call me blessed:
    the Almighty has done great things for me,
    and holy is his Name.
    He has mercy on those who fear him
    in every generation.
  He has shown the strength of his arm,
    and has scattered the proud in their conceit.
  He has cast down the mighty from their thrones,
    and has lifted up the lowly.
  He has filled the hungry with good things,
    and the rich he has sent away empty.
  He has come to the help of his servant Israel
    for he has remembered his promise of mercy,
    the promise he made to our fathers,
    to Abraham and his children for ever."

Mary remained with her about three months
  and then returned to her home.

The Gospel of the Lord.

August 19, 2007

TWENTIETH SUNDAY IN ORDINARY TIME

I have come not to establish peace, but rather division.

A reading from the holy Gospel according to Luke

12:49–53

Jesus said to his disciples:
  "I have come to set the earth on fire,
  and how I wish it were already blazing!
There is a baptism with which I must be baptized,
  and how great is my anguish until it is accomplished!
Do you think that I have come to establish peace
    on the earth?
No, I tell you, but rather division.
From now on a household of five will be divided,
  three against two and two against three;
  a father will be divided against his son
  and a son against his father,
  a mother against her daughter
  and a daughter against her mother,

a mother-in-law against her daughter-in-law
and a daughter-in-law against her mother-in-law."

The Gospel of the Lord.

August 26, 2007

TWENTY-FIRST SUNDAY IN ORDINARY TIME

They will come from east and west and recline at table in the kingdom of God.

A reading from the holy Gospel according to Luke   *13:22–30*

Jesus passed through towns and villages,
    teaching as he went and making his way to Jerusalem.
Someone asked him,
"Lord, will only a few people be saved?"
He answered them,
    "Strive to enter through the narrow gate,
    for many, I tell you, will attempt to enter
    but will not be strong enough.
After the master of the house has arisen and locked
        the door,
    then will you stand outside knocking and saying,
    'Lord, open the door for us.'
He will say to you in reply,
    'I do not know where you are from.'

And you will say,
  'We ate and drank in your company and you taught
    in our streets.'
Then he will say to you,
  'I do not know where you are from.
Depart from me, all you evildoers!'
And there will be wailing and grinding of teeth
  when you see Abraham, Isaac and Jacob
  and all the prophets in the kingdom of God
  and you yourselves cast out.
And people will come from the east and the west
  and from the north and the south
  and will recline at table in the kingdom of God.
For behold, some are last who will be first,
  and some are first who will be last."

The Gospel of the Lord.

September 2, 2007

Twenty-second Sunday in Ordinary Time

Everyone who exalts himself will be humbled, everyone who humbles himself will be exhalted.

A reading from the holy Gospel according to Luke 14:1, 7-14

On a sabbath Jesus went to dine
    at the home of one of the leading Pharisees,
    and the people there were observing him carefully.

He told a parable to those who had been invited,
    noticing how they were choosing the places of honor
        at the table.
"When you are invited by someone to
        a wedding banquet,
    do not recline at table in the place of honor.
A more distinguished guest than you may have been
        invited by him,
    and the host who invited both of you may approach
        you and say,
    'Give your place to this man,'
    and then you would proceed with embarrassment
    to take the lowest place.
Rather, when you are invited,
    go and take the lowest place
    so that when the host comes to you he may say,
    'My friend, move up to a higher position.'

Then you will enjoy the esteem of your companions at
    the table.
For every one who exalts himself will be humbled,
    but the one who humbles himself will be exalted."
Then he said to the host who invited him,
    "When you hold a lunch or a dinner,
    do not invite your friends or your brothers
    or your relatives or your wealthy neighbors,
    in case they may invite you back and you
      have repayment.
Rather, when you hold a banquet,
    invite the poor, the crippled, the lame, the blind;
    blessed indeed will you be because of their inability
      to repay you.
For you will be repaid at the resurrection of
    the righteous."

The Gospel of the Lord.

September 9, 2007

Twenty-third Sunday in Ordinary Time

Anyone of you who does not renounce all possessions cannot be my disciple.

A reading from the holy Gospel according to Luke 14:25–33

Great crowds were traveling with Jesus,
   and he turned and addressed them,
   "If anyone comes to me without hating his father
      and mother,
   wife and children, brothers and sisters,
   and even his own life,
   he cannot be my disciple.
Whoever does not carry his own cross and come after me
   cannot be my disciple.
Which of you wishing to construct a tower
   does not first sit down and calculate the cost
   to see if there is enough for its completion?
Otherwise, after laying the foundation
   and finding himself unable to finish the work
   the onlookers should laugh at him and say,
   'This one began to build but did not have the
      resources to finish.'
Or what king marching into battle would not first
      sit down
   and decide whether with ten thousand troops

he can successfully oppose another king
 advancing upon him with twenty thousand troops?
But if not, while he is still far away,
 he will send a delegation to ask for peace terms.
In the same way,
 anyone of you who does not renounce all
  his possessions
 cannot be my disciple."

The Gospel of the Lord.

September 16, 2007

TWENTY-FOURTH SUNDAY IN ORDINARY TIME

There will be great joy in heaven over one sinner who repents.

A reading from the holy Gospel according to Luke
15:1–10

Tax collectors and sinners were all drawing near
 to listen to Jesus,
 but the Pharisees and scribes began to complain,
  saying,
 "This man welcomes sinners and eats with them."

So to them he addressed this parable.
"What man among you having a hundred sheep
 and losing one of them

would not leave the ninety-nine in the desert
   and go after the lost one until he finds it?
And when he does find it,
   he sets it on his shoulders with great joy
   and, upon his arrival home,
   he calls together his friends and neighbors
      and says to them,
   'Rejoice with me because I have found my lost sheep.'
I tell you, in just the same way
   there will be more joy in heaven over one sinner
      who repents
   than over ninety-nine righteous people
   who have no need of repentance.

"Or what woman having ten coins and losing one
   would not light a lamp and sweep the house,
   searching carefully until she finds it?
And when she does find it,
   she calls together her friends and neighbors
   and says to them,
   'Rejoice with me because I have found the coin
      that I lost.'
In just the same way, I tell you,
   there will be rejoicing among the angels of God
   over one sinner who repents."

The Gospel of the Lord.

Shorter form

September 23, 2007

Twenty-fifth Sunday in Ordinary Time

You cannot serve both God and mammon.

A reading from the holy Gospel according to Luke
16:10–13

Jesus said to his disciples,
The person who is trustworthy in very small matters
   is also trustworthy in great ones;
   and the person who is dishonest in very small matters
   is also dishonest in great ones.
If, therefore, you are not trustworthy with
      dishonest wealth,
   who will trust you with true wealth?
If you are not trustworthy with what belongs to another,
   who will give you what is yours?
No servant can serve two masters.
He will either hate one and love the other,
   or be devoted to one and despise the other.
You cannot serve both God and mammon."

The Gospel of the Lord.

Shorter form

September 30, 2007

Twenty-sixth Sunday in Ordinary Time

You received what was good, Lazarus what was bad; now he is comforted, whereas you are tormented.

A reading from the holy Gospel according to Luke 16:19–31

Jesus said to the Pharisees:
"There was a rich man who dressed in purple garments
   and fine linen
and dined sumptuously each day.
And lying at his door was a poor man named Lazarus,
   covered with sores,
who would gladly have eaten his fill of the scraps
that fell from the rich man's table.
Dogs even used to come and lick his sores.
When the poor man died,
he was carried away by angels to the bosom
   of Abraham.
The rich man also died and was buried,
and from the netherworld, where he was in torment,
he raised his eyes and saw Abraham far off
and Lazarus at his side.
And he cried out, 'Father Abraham, have pity on me.
Send Lazarus to dip the tip of his finger in water and
   cool my tongue,
for I am suffering torment in these flames.'

"Abraham replied,
  'My child, remember that you received
  what was good during your lifetime
  while Lazarus likewise received what was bad;
  but now he is comforted here, whereas you
      are tormented.
Moreover, between us and you a great chasm
      is established
  to prevent anyone from crossing who might wish to go
  from our side to yours or from your side to ours.'
He said, 'Then I beg you, father,
  send him to my father's house, for I have five brothers,
  so that he may warn them,
  lest they too come to this place of torment.'
But Abraham replied, 'They have Moses and
      the prophets.
Let them listen to them.'
He said, 'Oh no, father Abraham,
  but if someone from the dead goes to them, they
      will repent.'
Then Abraham said, 'If they will not listen to Moses
      and the prophets,
  neither will they be persuaded if someone should rise
      from the dead.'"

The Gospel of the Lord.

October 7, 2007

Twenty-seventh Sunday in Ordinary Time

If you have faith!

A reading from the holy Gospel according to Luke

17:5–10

The apostles said to the Lord, "Increase our faith."
The Lord replied,
"If you have faith the size of a mustard seed,
    you would say to this mulberry tree,
    'Be uprooted and planted in the sea,' and it would
        obey you.

"Who among you would say to your servant
    who has just come in from plowing or tending sheep
        in the field,
    'Come here immediately and take your place at table'?
Would he not rather say to him,
    'Prepare something for me to eat.
Put on your apron and wait on me while I eat and drink.
You may eat and drink when I am finished'?
Is he grateful to that servant because he did what
        was commanded?
So should it be with you.

When you have done all you have been commanded,
   say, 'We are unprofitable servants;
   we have done what we were obliged to do.'"

The Gospel of the Lord.

October 14, 2007

Twenty-eighth Sunday in Ordinary Time

None but this foreigner has returned to give thanks to God.

A reading from the holy Gospel according to Luke
17:11–19

As Jesus continued his journey to Jerusalem,
   he traveled through Samaria and Galilee.
As he was entering a village, ten lepers met him.
They stood at a distance from him and raised their
     voices, saying,
   "Jesus, Master! Have pity on us!"
And when he saw them, he said,
   "Go show yourselves to the priests."
As they were going they were cleansed.
And one of them, realizing he had been healed,
   returned, glorifying God in a loud voice;
   and he fell at the feet of Jesus and thanked him.
He was a Samaritan.

Jesus said in reply,
  "Ten were cleansed, were they not?
Where are the other nine?
Has none but this foreigner returned to give thanks
    to God?"
Then he said to him, "Stand up and go;
  your faith has saved you."

The Gospel of the Lord.

October 21, 2007

TWENTY-NINTH SUNDAY IN ORDINARY TIME

God will secure the rights of his chosen ones who call out to him.

A reading from the holy Gospel according to Luke

18:1–8

Jesus told his disciples a parable
  about the necessity for them to pray always
    without becoming weary.
He said, "There was a judge in a certain town
  who neither feared God nor respected any
    human being.
And a widow in that town used to come to him and say,
  'Render a just decision for me against my adversary.'
For a long time the judge was unwilling, but eventually
  he thought,

'While it is true that I neither fear God nor respect
   any human being,
because this widow keeps bothering me
I shall deliver a just decision for her
lest she finally come and strike me.'"
The Lord said, "Pay attention to what the dishonest
   judge says.
Will not God then secure the rights of his chosen ones
   who call out to him day and night?
Will he be slow to answer them?
I tell you, he will see to it that justice is done for
   them speedily.
But when the Son of Man comes, will he find faith
   on earth?"

The Gospel of the Lord.

October 28, 2007

THIRTIETH SUNDAY IN ORDINARY TIME

The tax collector, not the Pharisee, went home justified.

A reading from the holy Gospel according to Luke
18:9–14

Jesus addressed this parable
  to those who were convinced of their
    own righteousness
  and despised everyone else.
"Two people went up to the temple area to pray;
  one was a Pharisee and the other was a tax collector.
The Pharisee took up his position and spoke this prayer
    to himself,
  'O God, I thank you that I am not like the rest
    of humanity—
  greedy, dishonest, adulterous—or even like this
    tax collector.
I fast twice a week, and I pay tithes on my
    whole income.'
But the tax collector stood off at a distance
  and would not even raise his eyes to heaven
  but beat his breast and prayed,
  'O God, be merciful to me a sinner.'
I tell you, the latter went home justified, not
    the former;

for whoever exalts himself will be humbled,
and the one who humbles himself will be exalted."

The Gospel of the Lord.

November 1, 2007

ALL SAINTS

Rejoice and be glad, for your reward will be great in heaven.

A reading from the holy Gospel according to Matthew

5:1–12a

When Jesus saw the crowds, he went up the mountain,
   and after he had sat down, his disciples came to him.
He began to teach them, saying:

"Blessed are the poor in spirit,
   for theirs is the Kingdom of heaven.
Blessed are they who mourn,
   for they will be comforted.
Blessed are the meek,
   for they will inherit the land.
Blessed are they who hunger and thirst for righteousness,
   for they will be satisfied.
Blessed are the merciful,
   for they will be shown mercy.
Blessed are the clean of heart,
   for they will see God.

Blessed are the peacemakers,
   for they will be called children of God.
Blessed are they who are persecuted for the sake
      of righteousness,
   for theirs is the Kingdom of heaven.
Blessed are you when they insult you and persecute you
   and utter every kind of evil against you falsely
      because of me.
Rejoice and be glad,
   for your reward will be great in heaven."

The Gospel of the Lord.

November 4, 2007

THIRTY-FIRST SUNDAY IN ORDINARY TIME

The Son of Man has come to seek and to save what was lost.

A reading from the holy Gospel according to Luke

19:1–10

At that time, Jesus came to Jericho and intended
      to pass through the town.
Now a man there named Zacchaeus,
   who was a chief tax collector and also a wealthy man,
   was seeking to see who Jesus was;
      but he could not see him because of the crowd,
      for he was short in stature.

So he ran ahead and climbed a sycamore tree in order to
    see Jesus,
  who was about to pass that way.
When he reached the place, Jesus looked up and said,
  "Zacchaeus, come down quickly,
  for today I must stay at your house."
And he came down quickly and received him with joy.
When they all saw this, they began to grumble, saying,
  "He has gone to stay at the house of a sinner."
But Zacchaeus stood there and said to the Lord,
  "Behold, half of my possessions, Lord, I shall give to
    the poor,
  and if I have extorted anything from anyone
  I shall repay it four times over."
And Jesus said to him,
  "Today salvation has come to this house
  because this man too is a descendant of Abraham.
For the Son of Man has come to seek
  and to save what was lost."

The Gospel of the Lord.

November 11, 2007

THIRTY-SECOND SUNDAY IN ORDINARY TIME

He is not God of the dead, but of the living.

A reading from the holy Gospel according to Luke
20:27, 34–38

Some Sadducees, those who deny that there is
   a resurrection,
   came forward.

Jesus said to them,
   "The children of this age marry and remarry;
   but those who are deemed worthy to attain to
      the coming age
   and to the resurrection of the dead
   neither marry nor are given in marriage.
They can no longer die,
   for they are like angels;
   and they are the children of God
   because they are the ones who will rise.
That the dead will rise
   even Moses made known in the passage about
      the bush,
   when he called out 'Lord,'
   the God of Abraham, the God of Isaac, and the God
      of Jacob;

and he is not God of the dead, but of the living,
for to him all are alive."

The Gospel of the Lord.

Shorter form

November 18, 2007

THIRTY-THIRD SUNDAY
IN ORDINARY TIME

By your perseverance you will secure your lives.

A reading from the holy Gospel according to Luke
21:5–19

While some people were speaking about
    how the temple was adorned with costly stones
        and votive offerings,
    Jesus said, "All that you see here—
    the days will come when there will not be left
    a stone upon another stone that will not be
        thrown down."

Then they asked him,
"Teacher, when will this happen?
And what sign will there be when all these things
    are about to happen?"
He answered,
"See that you not be deceived,

for many will come in my name, saying,
  'I am he,' and 'The time has come.'
Do not follow them!
When you hear of wars and insurrections,
  do not be terrified; for such things must happen first,
  but it will not immediately be the end."
Then he said to them,
"Nation will rise against nation, and kingdom
  against kingdom.
There will be powerful earthquakes, famines and plagues
  from place to place;
  and awesome sights and mighty signs will come from
  the sky.

"Before all this happens, however,
  they will seize and persecute you,
  they will hand you over to the synagogues and
  to prisons,
  and they will have you led before kings and governors
  because of my name.
It will lead to your giving testimony.
Remember, you are not to prepare your defense
  beforehand,
  for I myself shall give you a wisdom in speaking
  that all your adversaries will be powerless to resist
  or refute.
You will even be handed over by parents, brothers,
  relatives and friends,
  and they will put some of you to death.

You will be hated by all because of my name,
  but not a hair on your head will be destroyed.
By your perseverance you will secure your lives."

The Gospel of the Lord.

November 25, 2007

Our Lord Jesus Christ the King/ Thirty-fourth Sunday in Ordinary Time

Lord, remember me when you come into your kingdom.

A reading from the holy Gospel according to Luke   23:35–43

The rulers sneered at Jesus and said,
  "He saved others, let him save himself
  if he is the chosen one, the Christ of God."
Even the soldiers jeered at him.
As they approached to offer him wine they called out,
  "If you are King of the Jews, save yourself."
Above him there was an inscription that read,
  "This is the King of the Jews."

Now one of the criminals hanging there reviled Jesus,
    saying,
  "Are you not the Christ?
Save yourself and us."

The other, however, rebuking him, said in reply,
  "Have you no fear of God,
  for you are subject to the same condemnation?
And indeed, we have been condemned justly,
  for the sentence we received corresponds to
    our crimes,
  but this man has done nothing criminal."
Then he said,
  "Jesus, remember me when you come into
    your kingdom."
He replied to him,
  "Amen, I say to you,
  today you will be with me in Paradise."

The Gospel of the Lord.

PATRON SAINTS

The saints and blesseds are our companions in prayer on our journey with Christ. Here we provide you with a list of health concerns and the saints chosen to intercede on a sick person's behalf before God the Father.

AILMENTS	SAINT(S)
A	
abdominal pains	Agapitus; Charles Borromeo; Emerentiana; Erasmus; Liborius
abortion, protection against	Catherine of Sweden
abuse victims	Adelaide; Agostina Pietrantoni; Fabiola; John Baptist de la Salle
AIDS patients	Aloysius Gonzaga; Therese of Lisieux; Peregrine Lazios
alcoholism	John of God; Martin of Tours; Matthias the Apostle; Monica; Urban of Langres
angina sufferers	Swithbert
appendicitis	Erasmus (Elmo)
apoplexy, apoplexies, stroke, stroke victims	Andrew Avellino; Wolfgang
arm pain; pain in the arms	Amalburga
B	
babies	The Holy Innocents; Maximus; Nicholas of Tolentino; Philip of Zell
bacterial disease and infection	Agrippina
barren women	Anthony of Padua; Felicity

barrenness, against	Agatha; Anne; Anthony of Padua; Casilda of Toledo; Felicity; Fiacre; Francis of Paola; Giles; Henry II; Margaret of Antioch; Medard; Philomena; Rita of Cascia; Theobald Roggeri
birth complications, against	Ulric
birth pains	Erasmus
blind people, blindness	Catald; Cosmas and Damian; Dunstan; Lawrence the Illuminator; Leodegarius; Lucy; Lutgardis; Odila; Parasceva; Raphael the Archangel; Thomas the Apostle
blood donors	Our Lady of the Thorns
bodily ills, illness, sickness	Alphais; Alphonsa of India; Angela Merici; Angela Truszkowska; Arthelais; Bathild; Bernadette of Lourdes; Camillus of Lellis; Catherine del Ricci; Catherine of Siena; Drogo; Edel Quinn; Elizabeth of the Trinity; Gerard of Villamagna; Germaine Cousin; Gorgonia; Hugh of Lincoln; Isabella of France; Jacinta Marto; John of God; Julia Billiart; Julia Falconieri; Juliana of Nicomedia; Louis IX; Louise de Marillac; Lydwina of Schiedam; Maria Bagnesi; Maria Gabriella; Maria Mazzarello; Marie Rose Durocher; Mary Ann de Paredes; Mary Magdalen of Pazzi; Michael the Archangel; Our Lady of Lourdes; Paula Frassinetti; Peregrine Laziosi; Philomena; Rafka Al-Rayes; Raphael; Romula; Syncletica; Teresa of Avila; Teresa Valse Pantellini; Terese of the Andes; Therese of Lisieux
breast cancer	Agatha; Aldegundis; Giles; Peregrine
breast disease, against	Agatha

breastfeeding women	Giles
broken bones	Drogo; Stanislaus Kostka

C

cancer patients; against cancer	Aldegundis; Giles; James Salomone; Peregrine Laziosi
child abuse victims	Alodia; Germaine Cousin; Lufthild; Nunilo
childbirth	Erasmus; Gerard Majella; Leonard of Noblac; Lutgardis; Margaret (or Marina) of Antioch; Raymond Nonnatus
childhood diseases	Aldegundis; Pharaildis
childhood intestinal diseases	Erasmus
children, convulsive	Guy of Anderlecht; John the Baptist; Scholastica
children, death of	Alphonsa Hawthorne; Angela of Foligno; Clotilde; Conception Cabrera de Annida; Cyriacus of Iconium; Dorothy of Montau; Elizabeth of Hungary; Elizabeth Ann Seton; Felicity; Frances of Rome; Hedwig; Isidore the Farmer; Joaquina Vedruna de Mas; Julitta; Leopold the Good; Louis IX; Luchesius; Margaret of Scotland; Marguerite d'Youville; Matilda; Melania the Younger; Michelina; Nonna; Perpetua; Stephen of Hungary
children, sick	Beuno; Clement I; Hugh of Lincoln; Ubaldus Baldassini
children, stammering	Notkar Balbulus
colic	Agapitus; Charles Borremo; Emerentiana; Erasmus; Liborius
contagious diseases	Robert Bellarmine; Sebastian
consumption	Pantaleon; Therese of Liseux
convulsions	John the Baptist; Willibrord

coughs, against	Blaise; Quentin; Walburga
cramps, against	Cadoc of Llancarvan; Maurice; Pancras
cures from pain	Madron

D

deaf people, deafness	Cadoc of Llancarvan; Drogo; Francis de Sales; Meriadoc; Ouen
death	Michael the Archangel; Margaret (or Marina) of Antioch
death, happy	Joseph; Ulric
death, against sudden	Aldegundis; Andrew Avellino; Barbara; Christopher
disabled, handicapped	Alphais; Angela Merici; Gerald of Aurillac; Germaine Cousin; Giles; Henry II; Lutgardis; Margaret of Castello; Seraphina; Servatus; Servulus
drug abuse	Maximillian Kolbe
dying people, invoked by	Abel; Barbara; Benedict; Catherine of Alexandria; James the Lesser, Apostle; John of God; Joseph; Margaret (or Marina) of Antioch; Michael the Archangel; Nicholas of Tolentino; Sebastian
dysentary	Lucy of Syracuse; Polycarp

E

earache, against	Cornelius; Polycarp of Smyrna
epidemics	Godeberta; Lucy of Syracuse; Our Lady of Zapopan; Roch (Rocco)
epilepsy, epileptics	Alban of Mainz; Anthony the Abbot; Balthasar; Bibiana; Catald; Christopher; Cornelius; Dymphna; Genesius; Gerard of Lunel; Giles; Guy of Anderlecht; John

	Chrysostom; John the Baptist; Valentine; Vitus; Willibrord
ergotism, aginst	Anthony the Abbot
erysipelas	Anthony the Abbot; Benedict; Ida of Nivelles
expectant Mothers	Gerard Majella; Raymond Nonnatus
eyes, eye diseases, eye problems, sore eyes	Aloysius Gonzaga; Augustine of Hippo; Clare of Assisi; Cyriacus of Iconium; Erhard of Regensburg; Herve; Leodegarius; Lucy of Syracuse; Raphael the Archangel; Symphorian of Autun

F

fainting, faintness	Urban of Langres; Ursus of Ravenna; Valentine
fever, against	Abraham; Adalard; Amalberga; Andrew Abellon; Antoninus of Florence; Benedict; Castorus; Claudius; Cornelius; Dominic of Sora; Domitian of Huy; Four Crowned Martyrs; Genevieve; Gerebernus; Gertrude of Nivelles; Hugh of Cluny; Jodocus; Liborius; Mary of Oignies; Nicostratus; Peter the Apostle; Petronilla; Raymond Nonnatus; Severus of Avranches; Sigismund; Simpronian; Theobald Roggeri; Ulric; Winnoc
fistula	Fiacre
frenzy, against	Denis; Peter the Apostle; Ulric
foot problems; feet problems	Peter the Apostle; Servatus

G

gall stones	Benedict; Drogo; Florentius of Strasburg; Liborius

goiter	Blaise
gout, against; gout sufferers	Andrew the Apostle; Coloman; Gerebernus; Gregory the Great; Killian; Maurice; Maurus; Totman

H

hangovers	Bibiana
head injuries	John Licci
headaches	Acacius; Anastasius the Persian; Bibiana; Denis; Dionysius the Aeropagite; Gerard of Lunel; Gereon; Pancras; Stephen the Martyr; Teresa of Avila; William Firmatus
health	Infant Jesus of Prague
healthy throats	Andrew the Apostle; Blaise; Etheldreda; Godelieve; Ignatius of Antioch; Lucy of Syracuse; Swithbert
heart patients	John of God
hemorrhage	Lucy
hemorrhoid, piles	Fiacre
hernia	Alban of Mainz; Condrad Piacenzai; Cosmas and Damian; Drogo; Gummarus
herpes	George
hoarseness, against	Bernadine of Sienna; Maurus
hydrophobia (rabies)	Dominic de Silos; Guy of Anderlecht; Hubert of Liege; Otto of Bamberg; Sithney; Walburga

I

infertility, against	Agatha; Anne; Anthony of Padua; Casilda of Toledo; Felicity; Fiacre; Francis of Paola; Giles; Henry II; Margaret of

	Antioch; Medard; Philomena; Rita of Cascia; Theobald Roggeri
inflammatory disease	Benedict
intestinal diseases, against	Brice; Charles Borromeo; Emerentiana; Erasmus; Timonthy; Wolfgang
invalids, homebound	Roch (Rocco)

J

jauntice	Odilo

K

kidney disease, against	Benedict; Drogo; Margaret (or Marina) of Antioch; Ursus of Ravenna
kidney stones; gravel	Alban of Mainz
knee diseases or trouble	Roch (Rocco)

L

lame, the	Giles
leg diseases, leg trouble	Servatus
lepers, leprosy	George; Giles; Lazarus; Vincent de Paul
long life	Peter the Apostle
lumbago	Lawrence

M

mental illness	Benedict Joseph Labre; Bibiana; Christina the Astonishing; Drogo; Dymphna; Eustochium of Padua; Fillan; Giles; Job; Margaret of Cortona; Maria Fortunata Viti; Medard; Michelina; Osmund; Raphaela; Romanus of Condat; Veran
migraine	Gereon; Severus of Avranches; Ulbadus Baldassini

milk, loss of by nursing women	Margaret of Antioch
miscarriage, against	Catherine of Sienna; Catherine of Sweden; Eulalia
miscarriage prevention	Catherine of Sweeden
muteness	Drogo

N

near sightedness, short sightedness	Clarus; Abbot
nerve or neurological disease, against	Bartholomew the Apostle; Dymphna
nursing mothers	Concordia; Martina

O

obsession	Quirinus

P

pain relief	Madron
paralysis	Catald; Osmund; Wolfgang
physical spouse abuse, against; victims of spouse abuse, against:	Rita of Cascia
plague, against	Adrian of Nicomedia; Catald; Colman of Stockerau; Cuthbert; Edmund of East Anglia; Erhard of Regensburg; Francis of Paola; Francis Xavier; George; Genevieve; Gregory the Great; Macarius of Antioch; Roch (Rocco); Sebastian; Valentine; Walburga
poison sufferers	Benedict; Abbot; John the Apostles; Pirmin
pregnant women, pregnancy	Anne; Anthony of Padua; Elizabeth; Gerard Majella; Joseph; Margaret (or Marina) of Antioch; Raymond Nonnatus; Ulric

R

rape victims	Agatha; Agnes of Rome; Antona Messina; Dymphna; Joan of Arc; Maria Goretti; Pierina Morosini; Potamiaena; Solange; Zita
rheumatism, arthritis	Alphonus Maria de Liguori; Coloman; James the Greater; Killian; Servatus; Totnan
respiratory problems	Bernadine of Sienna
ruptures, against	Drogo; Florentius of Strasburg; Osmund

S

scrofulous diseases	Balbina; Marculf; Mark the Evangelist
skin disease	Anthony the Abbot; George; Marculf; Peregrine Laziosi; Roch (Rocco)
skin rashes	Anthony the Abbot; George; Marculf; Peregrine Laziosi; Roch (Rocco)
sleepwalkers, sleepwalking	Dymphna
smallpox	Matthias
snakebite victims	Hilary; Paul
spasms	John the Baptist
sterility, against	Agatha; Anne; Anthony of Padua; Casilda of Toledo; Felicity; Fiacre; Francis of Paola; Giles; Henry II; Margaret of Antioch; Medard; Philomena; Rita of Cascia; Theobald Roggeri
stillborn children	Edmund
stomach disease, stomach trouble	Brice; Charles Borromeo; Erasmus; Timothy; Wolfgang
stroke	Andrew Avellino; Wolfgang
struma	Balbina; Marculf; Mark the Evangelist
surgery patients	Infant of Prague

syphilis	Fiacre; George; Symphoroian of Autun

T

throat diseases, against	Andrew the Apostle; Blaise; Etheldreda; Godelieve; Ignatius of Antioch; Lucy of Syracuse; Swithbert
toothaches	Apollonia; Chirstopher; Elizabeth of Hungary; Ida of Nivelles; Kea; Medard; Osmund
tuberculosis	Pantaleon; Theresa of Liseaux
twitching, against	Bartholomew the Apostle; Cornelius
typhus, against; against typhoid	Adelard

U

ulcers, against	Charles Borromeo; Job

V

venereal disease	Fiacre
verbal spousal abuse	Anne Marie Taigi; Godelieve; Monica
vertigo, against	Ulric

W

whooping cough, against	Blaise; Winoc
women in labor	Anne; Erasmus; John of Bridlington; Margaret (or Marina) of Antioch; Margaret of Fontana; Mary of Oignies
women who wish to be mothers	Andrew the Apostle
wounds	Aldegundis; Marciana; Rita of Cascia